Information Technology

Policy and Strategy

The Workbook Edition

richard boateng

Information Technology Policy and Strategy
- *The Workbook Edition*

Copyright © 2017 Richard **Boateng**

This book was developed as part of the African Text Project. The project focuses on empowering African authors and academics in developing educational materials useful for teaching in African institutions.

RICHARD **BOATENG**
Email: richard@pearlrichards.org

CreateSpace Independent Publishing Platform
Charleston, USA.
eStore address (i.e. www.CreateSpace.com/ 6958915)
Printed by CreateSpace, An Amazon.com Company
CreateSpace, Charleston SC

ISBN-13: 978-1544115221
ISBN-10: 1544115229

To God Be The Glory

Just By Your Grace

To My Wife and Daughter

You Mean The World To Me

.

CONTENTS

List of Exhibits

Richard Boateng

Preface and Acknowledgments

You are welcome to Information Technology Policy and Strategy – Workbook Edition. The book aims at introducing readers to how organizations and institutions develop information systems strategies and corresponding policies to govern the development, deployment and use of information systems (IS). The objectives are to equip the reader/student with the knowledge and practice of strategic information systems planning and the implications new technologies have on their employees and the organisation as a whole. Through real-world case studies, the book enables the reader/student to evaluate the internal (e.g., processes, political and organizational culture) and external (e.g., laws, global concerns, and cultural issues) environments that organizations compete in and plan accordingly. It is aimed at being used in teaching and hence, it adopts an interactive approach requiring the reader/student to participate in the learning process.

On completion, the reader/student should be equipped to understand, assess and develop IS strategies and policies for organizations. The reader/student should also be able to evaluate new and emerging technologies to develop strategic plans on how they can be aligned with business processes and policies. Topics discussed in this book include information technology/policy development and implementation, strategic information systems planning, information strategy success, and information systems-business alignment. Topics are discussed alongside several global examples and case studies.

The book also features an overview of two strategic management theories, which are useful in analyzing the strategic behavior or decisions of firms. These theories - Resource-Based Theory (RBT) and Dynamic Capabilities (DC) Framework - have received much attention in strategic management and business studies, and are relevant in examining the strategic behavior of firms. RBT tends to be the prevailing paradigm that explains or helps to understand how and why firms develop the capability to gain and sustain competitive advantage. Within the two theories, rival firms are viewed to compete on the basis of their internal characteristics, resources, through which they build competitive advantage and a superior long-term performance.

Last but definitely not least, many thanks to my wife, Sheena Lovia Boateng, for her understanding, motivation and support. She is the inspiration for my writing and my life. Because of her, as wife, supporter, and detailed and careful editor, this work has been made possible. To our daughter, Astrid, Mum and Dad say, we love you!

Chapter 1 - Information Technology Policy in Organizations

The objective of this chapter is to enable readers/students understand and differentiate between information technology (IT) policy, standards and guidelines; enable students understand the basic types of IT policies required in organizations; and enable readers/students understand the relationship between policy and strategy.

DEFINING IT POLICY

Policies are high level statements which ensure or guide compliance. In relation to information systems (IS) or information technology (IS) strategy, policy may ensure compliance to the strategy. IT/IS policies articulate the firm's vision, strategy, and principles as they relate to the use of information and information technology resources. They tend to demonstrate a commitment from senior management to produce, responsibly manage and protect information and information-related resources. They outline

a. roles and responsibilities,

b. define the scope of information needed by the organization, and

c. provide a high level description of the controls that must be in place to facilitate the production and responsible usage of the information.

For example, regarding information systems security in an organization, an IS security policy, "outlines security roles and responsibilities, defines the scope of information to be protected, and provides a high level description of the controls that must be in place to protect information" [1].

Now, if we consider an educational institution, such as, The University of California – Santa Cruz, policies define how the university's Information Technology Services (ITS) unit will approach security, how employees (staff/faculty) and students are to approach security, and how certain situations regarding information security management and breaches will be handled.

IT/IS and Policy

Before we go any further into IT policy, let us go back and examine the basic question what is an information system or information technology.

An information system is an "arrangement of people, processes, and information technology that interact to collect, process, store, and provide as output the information needed to support an organization" [2]. Within an organization, an information system provides a solution to problem, a challenge, an opportunity for an organization and its consists of a combination information technology, business policy and structure, processes, and people. Information technology comprises the hardware and software a business uses to achieve objectives. Information and Communication Technologies (ICTs), another commonly used terminology, comprises the IT (hardware and software) and communication technologies (telecommunication devices).

IS = IT + People + Processes + Business Policy/Structure

IT = Hardware + Software + Network Infrastructure

As a result, if policies are governing mechanisms, then, an IS policy governs the appropriate use of information technology, business policy and structure, processes, and people to achieve and sustain organizational objectives. Similarly, IT policy governs the appropriate use of hardware, software and network infrastructure to achieve and sustain organizational objectives. IT/IS policies specify requirements and standards for the consistent use of IT resources across a firm. However, we need to appreciate that, IT and IS are sometimes used interchangeably, especially as technology is increasingly becoming pervasive and influencing every sphere of society.

Since organizations exist within a given society, industry or a country, which also has legal frameworks and policies to govern behavior of citizens, organizations, institutions and even government, IT/IS policies do not exist in vacuum. They should be developed incognizance of the context and nature of business operations and culture of an organization. IT/IS policies should therefore interpret applicable laws and regulations and ensure that the policies are consistent with legal and contractual requirements in an organization, industry and the country.

We also need to note that, as governing mechanisms, IT/IS policies may empower others whiles disempowering others. That's, policies can express expectations for acceptable or appropriate behavior, set the boundaries of acceptable behavior, and empower employees to do what they ought to be doing.

Practice Question 1

Should organizations have different policies for information systems and information technology or should the information technology policy be a subset, offshoot or related to the information systems policy? Discuss.

....

....

....

....

....

....

....

....

....

....

....

....

....

....

....

....

....

STANDARDS, GUIDELINES AND PROCEDURES

Standards/rules consist of specific **low level mandatory controls** that help enforce and support the information systems policy. Standards help to ensure consistency and coordination in the design, development, implementation and usage of information systems across the business. For example,

> A password **standard** may set out rules for password complexity which will be applicable for all user login interfaces.

Guidelines consist of **recommended, non-mandatory controls** that help support standards or serve as a reference when no applicable standard is in place. Guidelines should be viewed as best practices that are not usually requirements, but are strongly recommended. They could consist of additional recommended controls that support a standard, or help fill in the gaps where no specific standard applies. For example,

> A **standard** may require specific technical controls for accessing the internet securely and a separate **guideline** may outline the best practices for using the internet and managing your online presence.

Procedures are **specific operational steps** or **manual methods** to be followed in order to implement the goal of the written policies and standards. For example

> A **policy** could describe the need for backups, for storage off-site, and for safeguarding the backup media.

> A **standard/rule** could define the software to be used to perform backups and how to configure this software. A **guideline** may outline the best practices in performing backup, especially with the use of the software.

> A **procedure** could describe how to use the backup software, the timing for making backups, and other ways that users can interact with the backup system.

Policies are intended to last for longer time, say up to five years, while standards are intended to last only a few years. Standards will need to be changed considerably more often than policies because the manual procedures, organizational structures, business processes, and information technologies mentioned in standards change so rapidly. For example, a network security standard might specify that all new or substantially modified systems must be in compliance with International Standards Organization (ISO) standard X.509, which involves authentication of a secure communications channel through public key cryptography. This standard is likely to be revised or replaced in the next few years.

Now, let us examine a real world case example from Western Michigan University. The university has an Office of Information Technology responsible for managing and communicating IT related policies and rules (Exhibit 1).

Exhibit 1 Western Michigan University **Information Technology Rules and Policies**

The policy and communications unit of the office of information technology facilitates the development of information technology policies, rules, guidelines and procedures. The unit participates with the campus security committee as well as other University constituents to develop, implement and maintain University-level IT policies and works to educate the campus community on matters of policy, law, and best practices when accessing and using electronic data. Comments regarding the material found in the categories defined below should be directed to #######@wmich.edu.

DOCUMENT DEFINITIONS

Policy: A document that communicates compliance in matters as they pertain to the University's data and computing assets. IT policies are initiated by the campus information security committee or brought forth by other constituents of the University community. Policies are intended to be dynamic and require annual review in order to maintain relevance with best practices.

Rule: Similar to a policy but intended to describe the operations, definitions, and constraints of the use of computing resources.

Guidelines: Recommended actions and operational guides for users of systems and resources. Guidelines are created collaboratively with subject matter experts from various computing support units throughout the University. Guidelines incorporate best practices.

Procedures: Tasks that should be performed to achieve a desired outcome. Procedures can be created by central IT or departmental groups [3].

Practice Question 2

In reference to Exhibit 1, answer the following questions:

a) What is the role of the policy and communications unit of the office of IT?

....

....

....

....

....

....

....

....

In reference to Exhibit 1, answer the following questions:

b) Who are the stakeholders of the policies and rules?

....

....

....

....

In reference to Exhibit 1, answer the following questions:

c) How are policies developed and how are they maintained?

....

....

....

....

....

....

....

In reference to Exhibit 1, answer the following questions:

d) What are the interrelationships between polices, rules, guidelines and procedures?

....

....

....

....

....

....

....

....

....

....

....

....

....

....

....

....

....

IT POLICY AND IT STRATEGY

To explore the interrelationships between policy and strategy, we will review how different organizations and institutions across the world differentiate the two concepts and develop and implement/use them to achieve and sustain their objectives.

Exhibit 2 Support and Information Zone, University of Chichester

Strategy

The Digital and IT Strategy sets the direction for the development of Information Technology Services within the University. Our vision is to embrace the best of technology to ensure that every student will have an outstanding learning experience. The IT Strategy has been developed to support the University's 2020 Vision, enabling us to embrace the latest technologies and techniques across the education landscape in a way that is coherent with our strategic direction. This strategy sets out our aims to exploit digital technologies, to allow our staff and students to succeed in the digital world today and in the future.

Policy

IT services and facilities are provided to enable staff and students to carry out their work, research or studies while at the University. Authorisation to access these services is given on condition that the user complies with the University of Chichester's Electronic Information Security Policy and the Data Protection Policy. The policies guiding behavior are:

a. Electronic Information Security Policy 2016
b. The IT Code of Conduct
c. IT Provisioning Policy
d. Mobile Phones - Purchasing and Use Policy
e. University of Chichester Data Protection Policy
f. University requirements for sharing email accounts (generic accounts)
g. Best practice guidelines for SharePoint sites
h. Equipment Loans Terms and Conditions

Source: [4]

Practice Question 3

In reference to Exhibit 2, answer the following questions:

a) What is the relationship between IT strategy and the core vision of strategic direction of the university?

....

....

....

....

....

....

....

....

....

....

....

....

....

....

....

....

....

In reference to Exhibit 2, answer the following questions:

b) What is the relationship between IT strategy and IT policy?

....

....

....

....

....

....

....

....

....

....

....

....

....

....

....

....

....

Difference between Policy and Strategy

Exhibit 3 Certified Information Systems Auditor Examination

Policies are high-level documents developed by management to transmit its guiding **strategy** and philosophy to employees. Policies define, detail, and specify what is expected from employees and how management intends to meet the needs of customers, employees, and stakeholders. Policies can be developed internally, or can be based on international standards such as Common Criteria (A framework used to specify security requirements) or ISO 17799 (best practice recommendations for implementing good security management) [5].

In summary, a policy is governing mechanism - what is, or what is not done. While a strategy is the methodology used to achieve an objective or goal as prescribed by a policy. Policy formulation is responsibility of top level management. However, it could be initiated by middle management, but it would only come into effect after top management approval. While strategy formulation is basically done by middle level management and may also include top management. Policy is concerned with both thought, behavior and actions. While strategy is concerned primarily with action.

ROLE OF POLICY

Gregg [5] outlines three key objectives or roles of policies/standards/guidelines in an organizational context, namely:

- **Regulatory** – Policies ensure that the set of organizational governing mechanisms (policies, standards/rules, guidelines and procedures) are in accordance with laws and regulations of the industry, community, and nation.

- **Advisory** – Policies advise or educate stakeholders (employees, customers or students) on what is acceptable and what is not acceptable, and the consequences of unacceptable behavior or action. An example of an advisory policy is one covering acceptable use of the email. This policy might state that employees should use corporate email addresses for only business related transactions or communication; if they violate the policy, it could lead to disciplinary action or dismissal.

- **Informative** – Beyond enforcement and education, policies may be used to inform stakeholders (employees, customers or students). An example of a purchase return policy for an online retail shop is an example of an informative policy (see Exhibit 4).

Exhibit 4 Amazon.com Returns Policies

Amazon.com and most sellers on Amazon.com offer returns for items within 30 days of receipt of shipment.

Holiday Return Policy

Items shipped by Amazon.com between November 1, 2016 and December 31, 2016, may be returned until January 31, 2017, for a full refund, subject to our other return guidelines listed below. Items shipped from sellers other than Amazon.com are subject to this same holiday return policy unless otherwise stated in the seller's individual Return Policy. For more details on policies for items not shipped by Amazon.com, see Seller Returns Policies below.

Amazon.com Return Policy

Items shipped from Amazon.com, including Warehouse Deals, can be returned within 30 days of receipt of shipment in most cases. Some products have different policies or requirements associated with them.

Seller Return Policy

When you order from a seller that fulfills and ships its own inventory (also called a third party seller), your return will be sent back to the seller instead of Amazon.com. While most sellers offer a returns policy equivalent to Amazon.com's, some seller returns policies may vary. You can view the Seller's return policy before you purchase an item by viewing the Returns and Refunds Policy section of the Seller's profile page. Once you've ordered, you can select your order in the Online Returns Center, to view the seller's return policy.

Third party sellers must either provide a return address within the United States, provide a pre-paid return label, or offer a full refund without requesting the item be returned. If a seller does not offer these methods to return your items, you may file an A-to-z Guarantee claim to seek help with your return.

Source: [6]

Practice Question 4

In reference to Exhibit 4, outline the regulatory, advisory and informative roles of the Amazon's Returns Policy.

....

....

....

....

....

....

....

....

....

....

....

....

....

....

....

....

CHAPTER SUMMARY

The chapter has explained the relevance of IT/IS policy and explored the different governing mechanisms in organizations (policies, standards/rules, guidelines and procedures). We have learnt that a policy is governing mechanism - what is, or what is not done. While a strategy is the methodology used to achieve an objective or goal as prescribed by a policy. Standards/rules tend to be more specific than policies and are primarily developed and implemented at the tactical level (middle management). Standards are also mandatory, whiles guidelines, as best practices statements, within a policy are not mandatory. Procedures provide the steps for implementing standards and policies. All these governing mechanisms may be used for regulatory, advisory and informative purposes. Policies may be initiated by middle management but come into effect after top/senior management approval. Senior management use policies to express expectations for acceptable or appropriate behavior, set the boundaries of acceptable behavior, and empower employees to do what they ought to be doing.

Chapter 2 - Types and Examples of IT/IS Policies

The objective of this chapter is to enable readers/students understand and differentiate between the different types of IT/IS policies. The chapter also showcases examples of these policies to enable readers/students to understand the constituents of these policies and how the differ across organizations.

TYPES OF IT/IS POLICIES

There are several types of IT/IS policies which govern the appropriate and acceptable use of information technologies in organizations. In this chapter we will explore a number of them and also explore their constituents. Exhibits 5 – 7 illustrate different types of IT/IS policies.

Exhibit 5 Categories of IT/I Policies in Western Michigan University

Academic Applications
- Rules and policies applicable to academic applications

Copyright and Ethics
- Rules and best practices regarding legal use of information

Data Security
- Rules, policies and best practices regarding secure data

Email
- Rules and polices that govern use of email and email addresses at WMU

Identity Protection
- Information to help keep your digital identity secure

Miscellaneous
- Rules and policies to aid in adhering to computing resources best practices

Network and Internet
- Anti-virus and ethical use of network and computing resources

Web
- Policies and resource links for acceptable use of web resources and services

Exhibit 6 Systemwide IT Policies & Guidelines, University of California

Electronic Communications

Electronic Communications Policy (ECP)
APPLICABLE: SYSTEMWIDE
Establishes electronic communications
principles, rules and procedures for all
members of the UC community.

UC IT Accessibility Policy Link
APPLICABLE: SYSTEMWIDE
Establishes principles and requirements for
making UC's electronic environment
accessible to people with disabilities.

Legislative and Other Guidance

Handling FBI Requests
APPLICABLE: SYSTEMWIDE
Instructions for properly handling
information requests from the FBI or other
Federal agencies.

Federal Anti-Spam Law
APPLICABLE: SYSTEMWIDE
Guidelines for complying with the Federal
CAN-SPAM Act.

DMCA Guidelines
APPLICABLE: SYSTEMWIDE
Guidelines for the Digital Millennium
Copyright Act.

Information Security

Gramm-Leach-Bliley Compliance Plan
APPLICABLE: SYSTEMWIDE
Federal law to protect consumers'
personal financial information

**UC Business & Finance Bulletin: Electronic
Information Security (IS-3)**
APPLICABLE: SYSTEMWIDE
UC BFB IS-3 is the systemwide policy for
electronic information security.

**UC Information Security Breach Notification
Resources**
APPLICABLE: SYSTEMWIDE
Resources and guidelines for information
security incidents requiring notification.
Breach notification must be coordinated
with your Location's Chief Information
Security Officer and Counsel.

Records Management and Privacy

Records Management Policies (RMP)
APPLICABLE: SYSTEMWIDE
The UC Business and Finance Records
Management and Privacy (RMP) Bulletin
series establishes systemwide policies on
records management and information
privacy.

Protection of Personal Information
APPLICABLE: SYSTEMWIDE
Resources and guidance for protecting
personal information.

Exhibit 6 Systemwide IT Policies & Guidelines, University of California (continued)

Records Management and Privacy (continued)

ABCs of Privacy & Public Records
APPLICABLE: SYSTEMWIDE
A high level overview of public records and privacy at UC. The document is provided by the UC Office of General Counsel.

Sample Privacy Statement
APPLICABLE: SYSTEMWIDE
Basic privacy statement template for UC websites that collect personal information.

Web Site Privacy Policies
APPLICABLE: SYSTEMWIDE
Guidance provided by the UC Office of General Counsel on the California Online Privacy Protection Act (COPPA) and how it applies to the University of California

Local IT Policies

Local IT Policies focus on the different campuses - Berkeley, Davis, Irvine, Lawrence Berkeley National Lab, Los Angeles, Merced, Riverside, San Diego, San Francisco, Santa Barbara, Santa Cruz.

A campuswide policy meets one or both of the following criteria:
- It affects a broad range of the campus community, either because it is of general interest or applicability, or because one control unit establishes a set of principles and procedures that other control units must abide by;
- It coordinates compliance with applicable laws and regulations across control units, promotes operational consistency and efficiency, and/or reduces institutional risks.

Source: [3]

Exhibit 7 University of California Office of the President IT Policies & Guidelines

Acceptable Use

Acceptable Use of UCOP Electronic Information Resources
APPLICABLE: UCOP

UCOP User Agreement Form
APPLICABLE: UCOP
Information about the UCOP User Agreement form. The form must be signed by UCOP employees.

Electronic Communications

Electronic Message Management at UCOP
APPLICABLE: UCOP
Information and resources to assist UCOP staff in managing email.

Use of E-mail at UCOP
APPLICABLE: UCOP
Information and guidance on the proper use of email at UCOP.

UCOP Access with Consent Form
APPLICABLE: UCOP
Form to gain access to UCOP Electronic Communications Records when the Record Holder has given consent.

UCOP Access without Consent Form
APPLICABLE: UCOP
Form to gain access to UCOP Electronic Communications Records without the Record Holder's consent.

Requesting Access to An Employee's E-mail/Attachments or Computer Files: UCOP Procedure
APPLICABLE: UCOP
Procedures for UCOP staff to request access to a UCOP employee's electronic communications records such as email and computer files.

Applications

Use of Shibboleth/UCTrust Authentication for UCOP Applications
APPLICABLE: UCOP

Network

Security Requirements for All UCOP Networked Devices
APPLICABLE: UCOP

Minimum Standards for UCOP Network
APPLICABLE: UCOP

Terms & Conditions for Use of UCOP Data Network Services
APPLICABLE: UCOP

Source: [7]

Exhibit 7 University of California Office of the President IT Policies & Guidelines (continued)

Information Security

UCOP Electronic Information Security Policy
   APPLICABLE: UCOP
Establishes UCOP Electronic Information Security policy as required by UC Business and Finance Bulletin IS-3: Electronic Information Security.

User Account Management Guidance for UCOP Departments
   APPLICABLE: UCOP
UCOP guidelines for managing user accounts.

UCOP Information Security Breach Notification
   APPLICABLE: UCOP
Resources and information to assist in UCOP breach notification. UCOP breach notifications must be coordinated with UCOP's Chief Information Security Officer.

Passwords

UCOP Active Directory Password Standard
   APPLICABLE: UCOP
Password standard for UCOP's Active Directory

UCOP Linux Password Standard
   APPLICABLE: UCOP

Source: [7]

Practice Question 5

Identify the core categories of IT/IS policies in the two universities (see Exhibit 2, 5, 6 & 7). Tick as it may apply.

Category	University of Chichester	Univ. of West. Michigan	University of California
1.			
2.			
3.			
4.			
5.			
6.			
7.			
8.			
9.			
10.			
11.			
12.			
13.			
14.			
15.			
16.			

Practice Question 6

Provide descriptions to explain the different categories of
IT/IS policies identified in practice question 5.

Category	Description
1.	
2.	
3.	
4.	
5.	
6.	
7.	
8.	
9.	
10.	

Category	Description
11.	
12.	
13.	
14.	
15.	
16.	

Practice Question 7

The word 'APPLICABLE' is used repeatedly in the description of the IT/IS policies of University of California. What does it mean?

....

....

....

....

....

....

....

Exhibit 8 IT/IS Related Policies of Highland Bank

Information Security Policy

At Highland Bank your privacy and security is important to us. All transmissions between your computer and our computer network are encrypted using industry standard protocols. In order to access your account information and to transact business using our Internet Banking system you must have both an AccessID and Password. In addition, some business applications require the use of a token for additional security.

ID Theft Policy

Highland Bank maintains internal controls sufficient to protect customer financial information as outlined in our Information Security Policy and procedures.

Privacy Statement

As a customer of Highland Bank, we place the highest priority on safeguarding any and all financial information you provide us. Because you trust us with your financial and other personal information, we respect your privacy and safeguard your information. We take every precaution to keep your information confidential. It is our pledge to you. Please read our Privacy Statement or contact us with any questions regarding our use of your information.

Do Not Call Policy

Highland Bank respects the privacy of all consumers. If you would prefer not to receive consumer related direct marketing communications from Highland Bank, you need to request that your name be placed on Highland Bank's Do Not Call List and/or Highland Bank's Do Not Mail List.

Technical Requirements

To provide you the most effective and secure online access to Highland Bank accounts and services, we strongly recommend that you use or upgrade to the latest version of software supported by Highland Bank. These include browser requirements and PDF requirements.

External Link Disclaimer

Highland Bank has no control over information at any site hyperlinked to or from this Site. In no event shall Highland Bank be responsible for your use of a hyperlinked site. Highland Bank makes no representation concerning and is not responsible for the quality, content, nature, or reliability of any hyperlinked site and is providing this hyperlink to you only as a convenience. The inclusion of any hyperlink does not imply any endorsement, investigation, verification or monitoring by Highland Bank of any information in any hyperlinked site.

Source: [8]

GENERAL ORGANIZATIONAL POLICIES AND IT MANAGEMENT

Depending on the nature of operations of organizations, general policies governing business operations may also influence or affect the governance of IT/IS management. This is very evident in financial institutions. In Exhibit 8 (previous page), we can assess that Highland Bank's IT policies tend to govern activities directly related to the use of computer related transactions. These include information security, privacy and technical requirements. However, there is also Do Not Call Policy which addresses the respect of the privacy of all consumers. This policy has indirect effect on IT management. In implementing the policy, there is a need develop and maintain a database to support the marketing communications unit of bank. Hence, though it is not an IT/IS policy it has an indirect effect on IT management. As such, in the development of IT/IS policies, the chief technology officer of the bank has to consider the indirect effects of general policies.

Practice Question 8

General Policies of Community Banker University is summarized below. Evaluate the implications of these general polices on IT/IS management.

Policy	Description	Implications to IT/IS Management
E-Sign Act Policy	The E-Sign Act provides a general rule of validity for electronic records and signatures for transactions in or affecting interstate or foreign commerce. E-Sign allows the use of electronic records to satisfy any statute, regulation, or rule of law requiring that such information be provided in writing, if the consumer has affirmatively consented to such use and has not withdrawn such consent.	
Code of Conduct and Ethics Program	Guides compliance with the Bank Bribery Act. Sets forth the basic policies of ethical conduct, the foundation of basic business standards, and personal conduct.	
Internal and External Audit	Designed to assist board members with their audit responsibilities. Includes audit function structure and committee meetings, technical duties, compliance, filing audit reports, roles and responsibilities of the auditor, external audit firms, and review of external audit.	

Policy	Description	Implications to IT/IS Management
Internal Controls	Addresses the various controls to ensure efficient and effective bank operations, the reliability of financial reporting, and an effective risk management system. Covers administrative, accounting, and operating controls.	
Electronic Data Processing	Outlines the basic standards required to meet all areas of the bank's data processing operations. Provides structure and guidance to management, establishes controls, and addresses outside vendors, program security, and documentation.	
Overdrafts	Designed to address the risk associated with overdrafts, including the responsibility to communicate the policy to customers, payment or return of items, collection, charge-off and account closings, error resolution, and reporting.	
Wire Transfer	Identifies the risks and establishes the policies dealing with wire transfers. Covers how to accurately process requests made in person, by phone, or other electronic means, with emphasis on regulatory requirements, money laundering, and settlement by giving best practice examples.	
Dormant Accounts	Addresses responsibility, defining dormant/inactive accounts, processing, reporting, and service charges and interest payments.	
Marketing	Provides guidelines for the management of the bank's marketing function, including development of the annual marketing plan and ongoing decision making. Includes regulatory compliance, geographic limitations, and prohibited activities.	
Diversity and Inclusion	Diversity and inclusion standards have been set and this policy assists a financial institution in defining how it will implement, monitor, and convey their standards in the hiring and promoting of employees and in dealing with suppliers. Includes a policy statement suitable for public sharing.	

SANS Security Policy Information Security Policy

SANS Security Policy Resource page is a consensus research project of the SANS community. The ultimate goal of the project is to offer everything you need for rapid development and implementation of information security policies. The policies are categorized as:

Access all these policy templates at: https://www.sans.org/security-resources/policies

General

1. Acceptable Encryption Policy
2. Acceptable Use Policy
3. Clean Desk Policy
4. Data Breach Response Policy
5. Disaster Recovery Plan Policy
6. Digital Signature Acceptance Policy
7. Email Policy
8. Ethics Policy
9. Pandemic Response Planning Policy
10. Password Construction Guidelines
11. Password Protection Policy
12. Security Response Plan Policy
13. End User Encryption Key Protection Policy

Network Security

1. Acquisition Assessment Policy
2. Bluetooth Baseline Requirements Policy
3. Remote Access Policy
4. Remote Access Tools Policy
5. Router and Switch Security Policy
6. Wireless Communication Policy
7. Wireless Communication Standard

Access all these templates at: https://www.sans.org/security-resources/policies

Server Security

1. Database Credentials Policy
2. Technology Equipment Disposal Policy
3. Information Logging Standard
4. Lab Security Policy
5. Server Security Policy
6. Software Installation Policy
7. Workstation Security (For HIPAA) Policy

Application Security

- Web Application Security Policy

Old/Retired

1. Analog/ISDN Line Security Policy
2. Anti-Virus Guidelines
3. Server Audit Policy
4. Automatically Forwarded Email Policy
5. Communications Equipment Policy
6. Dial In Access Policy
7. Extranet Policy
8. Internet DMZ Equipment Policy
9. Internet Usage Policy
10. Mobile Device Encryption Policy
11. Personal Communication Devices and Voicemail Policy
12. Removable Media Policy
13. Risk Assessment Policy
14. Server Malware Protection Policy
15. Social Engineering Awareness Policy
16. DMZ Lab Security Policy
17. Email Retention Policy
18. Employee Internet Use Monitoring and Filtering Policy
19. Lab Antivirus Policy
20. Mobile Employee Endpoint Responsibility Policy
21. Remote Access Mobile Computing Storage
22. Virtual Private Network Policy

Access all these templates at: https://www.sans.org/security-resources/policies

EXAMPLES OF IT/IS POLICIES

Academic Applications - Classroom Technology: Standards (extract)

The following standards are for classrooms on all Western Michigan University campuses. This document shall be used in connection with any consulting pertaining to classroom technology projects. Outside consultants shall use this standard and adhere to the equipment listed herein to prepare all written bid documentation.

Level 1: General-use classroom designed for twenty to forty-nine students.
- General equipment list:
- Screen, manual, 16:10 format
- HD LCD projector, ceiling mounted
- Crestron touch panel (annotation optional)
- LCD input monitor
- Classroom technology station
- VOIP two-way Communication using Barix Annuncicom
- Three (3) Ethernet connections at cart. One (1) at projector.
- Crestron control system
- Blu-ray player
- HD Document camera
- Audio system (speakers and amplifiers)

AV Component Specifications
1. Screens
a) Screens shall be mounted flush with the ceiling or above the ceiling in rooms that have 8-foot ceilings. The bottom of the projected image should be no less than 38" off the floor.
b) Image size should be calculated using the following formula: For HDTV projection (16:9), Widescreen, 16:10, or 15:9 formats, screen height should equal 1/5 the distance from the screen to the furthest most seat or maximum height less than 38" from the floor.
c) Screens in level 1 and level 2 rooms are a 16:10, 72.5" x 116" manual screen. Level 3 rooms require a 16:10 ratio motorized screen.
d) Screen location is determined by locating the screen away from the teaching station. Use the center of the front of the room as a starting point for the edge of the screen. Imagine a 2-screen setup and remove the screen closet to the teaching station.

Source: [3]

Email Address Use and Rules

RUL 08-EM.01: Rule

Authority: Campus Information Security Group
History: First issued: DEC. 2012 Last revised: Dec. 2012 Last reviewed: Dec. 2012

Related policies: Mass email policy, Computing resources acceptable use policy
Additional references: Email rules

Contact information: Contact xxxxx@wmich.edu

PURPOSE
This document establishes rules for the use of the Western Michigan University email address.

SCOPE
This rule has been developed to encourage the use of official WMU email addresses for conducting official business of the University. The use of other email accounts (e.g., Yahoo, Gmail, AOL, Charter, SBC, etc.) to conduct official business with enrolled students is prohibited. This rule applies to all work-related email engaged in by all University employees, faculty, and staff. All such email communications must use the University's email system.

RULE STATEMENTS
- Email addresses are assigned at the time of Bronco NetID creation.
- Student email addresses are in the format of firstname-middle initial.lastname at wmich.edu.
- Faculty and staff email addresses are typically* in the format of firstname.lastname at wmich.edu.
- Only email sent to the University email address of record will be supported.
- Email may not be automatically forwarded to off-campus computer accounts from your University assigned email account.
- Email sent in the format of username at wmich.edu is not supported.
- All email sent from an administrative or academic office is considered to be an official notice and must contain a valid "to", "from", and "reply-to", and identify the person or process that initiated the message.
- Since some official communications may be time-sensitive, students, faculty and staff are responsible for reading their WMU email on a frequent and regular basis.

* Middle initials may be used in faculty or staff email addresses when more than one person exists with the same first and last names. Numbers will be added to any email addresses if more than one first, middle initial, and last name exists.

DEFINITIONS

WMU email address is the official email address assigned at the time one's Bronco NetID is created. Bronco NetID is a unique identifier that is automatically assigned when a student is admitted, or a faculty or staff member is hired. It remains active as long as enrollment, employment, or official University affiliation continues.

JUSTIFICATION

Western Michigan University uses email to communicate official University information of all kinds to students, faculty, and staff. If non-wmich.edu email addresses are used, and email is sent to ISP addresses, such as AOL, gmail, or hotmail, etc., and the person receiving the message from wmich.edu marks the message as spam, then a percentage of email sent to others with that ISP's address, from WMU is also blocked for a period of days. The percentage increase as the number of people marking the message as spam increases. This means that large numbers of WMU students or prospective students, would not receive official communications from WMU. It is therefore critical that all official email to WMU students, prospective students, faculty, or staff be sent to the official wmich.edu email address and from an official wmich.edu address.

ENFORCEMENT

Individuals who conduct official business for Western Michigan University shall abide by the rules of this policy. Any person found to be in violation of this policy, will be subject to appropriate disciplinary action as defined by current University policy.

REFERENCE

Email rules I Mass email policy I Computing resources acceptable use policy

DOCUMENT ACTION

Revised: Dec. 2012

Source: [3]

Other Information

These policies govern the use of email at Western Michigan University
Email address
- Rules about official WMU email addresses

Email
- Rules about appropriate use of WMU email

Mailing lists
- Obtaining and using WMU mailing lists

Mass email
- Who can send WMU mass emails

Mass email for research
- Rules for use of mass email for research at WMU

Password Policy

Employees at Company ABC must access a variety of IT resources, including computers and other hardware devices, data storage systems, and other accounts. Passwords are a key part of IT's strategy to make sure only authorized people can access those resources and data. All employees who have access to any of those resources are responsible for choosing strong passwords and protecting their log-in information from unauthorized people.

The purpose of this policy is to make sure all Company ABC resources and data receive adequate password protection. The policy covers all employees who are responsible for one or more account or have access to any resource that requires a password.

Password creation
- All passwords should be reasonably complex and difficult for unauthorized people to guess. Employees should choose passwords that are at least eight characters long and contain a combination of upper- and lower-case letters, numbers, and punctuation marks and other special characters. These requirements will be enforced with software when possible.
- In addition to meeting those requirements, employees should also use common sense when choosing passwords. They must avoid basic combinations that are easy to crack. For instance, choices like "password," "password1" and "Pa$$w0rd" are equally bad from a security perspective.
- A password should be unique, with meaning only to the employee who chooses it. That means dictionary words, common phrases and even names should be avoided. One recommended method to choosing a strong password that is still easy to remember: Pick a phrase, take its initials and replace some of those letters with numbers and other characters and mix up the capitalization. For example, the phrase "This may be one way to remember" can become "TmB0WTr!".
- Employees must choose unique passwords for all of their company accounts, and may not use a password that they are already using for a personal account.
- All passwords must be changed regularly, with the frequency varying based on the sensitivity of the account in question. This requirement will be enforced using software when possible.
- If the security of a password is in doubt– for example, if it appears that an unauthorized person has logged in to the account — the password must be changed immediately.
- Default passwords — such as those created for new employees when they start or those that protect new systems when they're initially set up — must be changed as quickly as possible.

Protecting passwords
- Employees may never share their passwords with anyone else in the company, including co-workers, managers, administrative assistants, IT staff members, etc. Everyone who needs access to a system will be given their own unique password.
- Employees may never share their passwords with any outside parties, including those claiming to be representatives of a business partner with a legitimate need to access a system.

- Employees should take steps to <u>avoid phishing scams</u> and other attempts by hackers to steal passwords and other sensitive information. All employees will receive training on how to recognize these attacks.
- Employees must refrain from writing passwords down and keeping them at their workstations. See above for advice on creating memorable but secure passwords.
- Employees may not use password managers or other tools to help store and remember passwords without IT's permission.

Source: [9]

Social Media Policy

Social matters. It matters for so many reasons. It largely currently underpins the communications strategy of a number of firms globally. Its growth has also been phenomenal. A compilation of the most popular social networks worldwide prepared by Statista gives a clear picture with Facebook holding an 18% market share having over 1,590 million active users, 7% more so than its closest competitor, the Facebook-owned, WhatsApp [10]. As a result, having a policy to manage the appropriate and acceptable usage of social media in the workplace or in business, cannot be overstated.

Entrepreneur [11] cites three key reasons to implement one:

1. Protect your company's reputation: "A social media policy takes the guesswork out of what is appropriate for employees to post about your company to their social networks."

2. Minimize confusion about murky legal issues: "Social media policies can also help entrepreneurs and managers avoid errors."

3. Raise awareness of your brand: "Too often organizations think about social media policies as a list of restrictions. But having clear guidelines can also help employees understand ways they can use social media to help achieve business goals. For instance, policies should advise employees how they can comment on blogs or social networks to boost brand awareness and drive traffic to the company's site."

Other key concerns highlighted by employers can be summarized as [12]:

1. **Misunderstanding**. It is unwise for employers to assume that employees will understand that the use of social media could be considered as a non-work activity. This has to be communicated clearly, especially with regard to what is and what is not acceptable.

2. **Employees Have Rights to Engage in Concerted Activity**. In countries such as the United States of America, labour regulations tend to communcate the fact that, employees have the right to engage in "concerted activity" for their "mutual aid and protection" about their terms and conditions of employment.

3. **Anonymous or Pseudonymous Posts**. Posts endorsing products and services could come from employees. This is not acceptable in countries like the United States of America. Employers are required to social media policies should prohibit

anonymous or pseudonymous activities by employees and to according to the Federal Trade Commission ("FTC"), the company is required to disclose a "material connection" about anyone who endorses or recommends a company's products or services.

4. **Harassment**. Employees will invariably talk to and about each other via social media. Hence, a social media policy has to define acceptable behaviour and conversation between and about employees on social media channels.

5. **Intellectual Property**. Employees post or disseminate the intellectual property of others without permission. An employer an employer could become subject to infringement claims or breach of contract claims. Hence, developing a social media policy, which employees, sign off may be needed to protect the employer.

6. **Private Information**. As mentioned in the previous points (5 and 6), employees may post private information about either employer or other employees, which could lead to a legal case. As such a social media policy may offer the protection for the employer.

7. **Recruiting and Hiring**. Employers could face legal issues when information from social media pages are used to influence recruitement and hiring decisions. There must be clear guidelines to inform human resource managers on how to use such information. Further, recruitment and hiring policies may be updated to address the role of social media information.

8. **Discipline vs Responsible Usage**. Employers are required to promote responsible usage of social media by employees, especially for organizational activities. Employers must intervene and impose discipline on employees who do anything to affect the legal status of the firm and commitment to its stakeholders. Such activities may include threatening, intimidating, or harassing customers, and other employees and revealing private or proprietary information.

Now, that we have a better understanding of why social media policy matters, let us explore examples from adidas and Thomson Reuters.

adidas Group Social Media Guidelines [13]

Our employer is easy to identify with and all of us are very passionate about what we do on a daily basis. At the adidas Group we believe in open communication and you are encouraged to tell the world about your work and share your passion. Whether you do so by participating in a blog, wiki, online social network or any other form of online publishing or discussion is completely up to you. However, these new ways of communication are changing the way we talk to each other and even to our consumers, target audiences and partners.

In order to avoid any problems or misunderstandings, we have come up with a few guidelines to provide helpful and practical advice for you when operating on the internet as an identifiable employee of the adidas Group and its brands.

1. First, please familiarize yourself with and follow the adidas Group Code of Conduct and the Global Policy Manuals.

2. When you discuss adidas Group- or brand-related matters on the internet, you must identify yourself with your name and, when relevant, your role at the adidas Group. Only very few people in this company are official spokesperson for the Group or its brands, so if you are not one of them you must make clear that you are speaking for yourself and not for the Group. You can use a disclaimer like "The postings on this site are my own and do not necessarily represent the position, strategy or opinions of the adidas Group and its brands". Please always write in the first person and don't use your company email address for private communications. And please consider that even anonymous postings on Wikipedia can be traced back to the company.

3. You are **personally responsible** for the content you publish on blogs, wikis or any other form of user-generated media. Please remember that the internet never forgets. This means everything you publish will be visible to the world for a very, very long time. **Common sense** is a huge factor here. If you are about to publish something that makes you even the slightest bit uncomfortable, review. If you are still unsure and it is related to the adidas Group and its brands, talk to your manager or Corporate Communications (please find contacts below).

4. Just because information is on the internal network (like the adiweb, das-net or Vision Asia), it is not ok to let the rest of the world know about it. If an item features the sentence "for internal use only" then that is exactly what it means and it is absolutely not meant to be forwarded to anyone who is not employed by the adidas Group. No exceptions. Messages from our CEO to all employees are not meant for the media. If we as a company wanted a newspaper to know how our CEO sees the future of our Group the PR department would call them up and tell them.

5. It is perfectly fine to talk about your work and have a dialogue with the community (see # 2) but it is not okay to talk about the design or name for the new World Cup ball months before its official launch. If you have signed a **confidentiality agreement** you are expected to follow it. If the judgement call is tough on secrets or other issues discussed, please ask your manager before you publish or forward. Please act responsibly with the information you are entrusted with.

6. **Do not comment** on work-related legal matters unless you are an official spokesperson, and have the legal approval by the adidas Group or its brands to do so. In addition, talking about revenues, future products, pricing decisions, unannounced financial results or similar matters will get you, the company or both into serious trouble. Stay away from discussing financial topics and predictions of future performance at all costs.

7. **Respect your audience.** Don't use ethnic slurs, personal insults, obscenity, or engage in any conduct that would not be acceptable in the adidas Group's workplace. You should also show proper consideration for others privacy and for topics that may be considered objectionable or inflammatory (like religion or politics). If you are in a virtual world as an adidas Group representative please dress and behave accordingly. We all appreciate respect.

8. **Think about consequences.** Imagine you are sitting in a sales meeting and your client brings out a printout of a colleague's post that states that the product you were about to sell "completely sucks". Talk about a tough pitch. So, please remember: Using your public voice to trash or embarrass your employer, your customers, your co-workers or even yourself is not okay - and not very smart.

9. Have you posted something that just wasn't true? **Be the first to respond to your own mistake.** In a blog, if you choose to modify an earlier post, make it clear that you have done so.

10. **Please respect copyright.** If it is not yours, don't use it. It is very simple. It is that person's choice to share his or her material with the world, not yours. Before posting someone else's work, please check with the owner first.

11. Don't cite or **reference** clients, partners or suppliers without their approval. When you do make a reference, where possible, link back to the source.

12. Be aware that others will **associate you with your employer** when you identify yourself as such. Please ensure that your Facebook, Linked-in, Xing or MySpace profile and related content is consistent with how you wish to present yourself with clients and colleagues.

13. Even if you act with the best **intentions**, you must remember that anything you put out there about the adidas Group can potentially harm the company. This goes for all internal media as well, like the intranet or any newsletters you send out. As soon as you act on

the company's behalf by distributing information, you are upholding the company's image. Please act responsibly. If in doubt, please contact the Corporate Communications Team (see contacts below) or your manager before you hit the send button.

14. And finally. With all the blogging and interacting, don't forget your daily job...

Reuters' Reporting from the Internet and Using Social Media [14]

We are committed to aggressive journalism in all its forms, including in the field of computer-assisted reporting, but we draw the line at illegal behaviour. Internet reporting is nothing more than applying the principles of sound journalism to the sometimes unusual situations thrown up in the virtual world. The same standards of sourcing, identification and verification apply. Apply the same precautions online that you would use in other forms of newsgathering and do not use anything from the Internet that is not sourced in such a way that you can verify where it came from.

No falsehoods

Reporters must never misrepresent themselves, including in chat rooms and other online discussion forums. They do not "pick locks" in pursuit of information, nor do they otherwise obtain information illegally. Discovering information publicly available on the web is fair game. Defeating passwords or other security methods is going too far.

Know your subject

Reporters should use aggressive Internet reporting techniques only when they are familiar with the way an organisation releases news. Familiarity with an organisation's past disclosure procedures can insulate us from all-too-common Internet spoofs. Please capture, save and print a copy of a screenshot" of the web page in question in order to defend us against charges of printing nonexistent information. If you do not know how to capture a screenshot, ask anyone with a technical bent to show you how. It is our best protection against vanishing web sites. Be wary of "unusual" news iscovered on a web site. Do not treat this as "normal news" until the company or organisation confirms it or at least has a chance to respond to what you have found. Escalate such situations to your manager. Also keep in mind what we consider newsworthy. Personal information must be relevant to a legitimate story for Reuters to publish it. Copyright laws, and libel laws, apply to the Internet too.

Attribution

Headlines should be very clear when we have obtained information in unorthodox settings. In stories, we also must make it clear high up how we gathered the information. Retain those facts high in the story as it plays out. The reader wants to know how we obtained the information.

Fairness

The act of seeking confirmation of the news before publishing it can lead the organisation to front-run our story and announce the information before we have a chance to put our story out. This does not relieve us of the responsibility to give an organisation a fair chance to comment. Please make it clear if the organisation is unwilling to confirm the information.

Is It A Hoax?

Do a reality check. Does this information fit within the bounds of what was expected? Any wild divergences are a clue you may be viewing information in the wrong context.

Using Social Media

We want to encourage you to use social media approaches in your journalism but we also need to make sure that you are fully aware of the risks -- especially those that threaten our hard-earned reputation for independence and freedom from bias or our brand. The recommendations below offer general guidance with more detailed suggestions for managing your resence on the most popular social networks. This is a fast-changing world and you will need to exercise judgment in many areas. In framing this advice we've borne in mind the following principles and encourage you to think about them whenever using social media.

Social Media: Basic Principles

Social networks have been a great boon for the practice of journalism, on stories large and small, and Reuters journalism has been the better for them. Not only have they served as a conduit for primary- and crowd-sourced information, they have also given us new ways to report -- "finding stories and tipsters on Twitter, using LinkedIn to locate sources, mining Facebook groups for angles and insights, and so on.

Social networks also raise important questions for us, especially when we are using them to transmit rather than receive. The issues around what we can and cannot say there are a subject of constant conversation among us, so as this is not our first word on the subject, it will not be the last. The online world is as full of pitfalls as it was when the Handbook was issued, but the issues are more familiar now, so it makes sense to simplify the guidelines.

Our wish is for people to benefit safely from social networks, not to muzzle anyone. Journalists are people too, with all the rights of citizens. If we want to tweet or post about a school play, a film or a favorite recipe, we are free to do so. When dealing with matters of public importance and actual or potential subjects of coverage, however, Reuters journalists should be mindful of the impact their publicly expressed opinions can have on their work and on Reuters. In our Twitter and Facebook profiles, for example, we should identify ourselves as Reuters journalists and declare that we speak for ourselves, not for Thomson Reuters.

When writing as Reuters journalists, whether for the file or online, we are guided 24 hours a day by the ethics of our organization as embodied in the Code of Conduct and the Trust Principles, which require us to be responsible, fair and impartial. On the one hand, these standards can be compromised whenever we "like" a post or adopt a "badge" or "join" a cause, particularly when the subject is relevant or even tangential to our beat. On the other hand, it might be necessary to "like," "join" or adopt a "badge" to get the news. It should go without saying that no one may compel or pressure anyone to friend them on Facebook, follow them on Twitter or engage in similar conduct on other social media. One of the distinguishing features of Reuters is the trust invested in the judgment of its journalists – and we will continue to look to our journalists to use their common sense in dealing with these new challenges.

We expect our journalists to reach conclusions through reporting, but they must also demonstrate the intellectual discipline to keep their conclusions susceptible to further reporting, which requires a posture of open-mindedness and enlightened skepticism. This is difficult to demonstrate in the social networks' short forms and under the pressure of thinking-writing-posting in real time. But maintaining this posture is critical to our credibility and reputation as journalists. When in doubt about a post, tweet or other action on social networks, we must enlist a second pair of eyes, even at the cost of some delay.

On matters dealing with Thomson Reuters, we must observe our existing obligations of confidentiality and the obvious boundaries of discretion—for example, refraining from the disclosure of inside information, confidential personnel matters, sensitive information from internal meetings (all of which are to be considered "off the record"). But nothing in this paragraph or in this policy should be interpreted as inhibiting the exchange of ideas about matters that deal with our common welfare. Nor is there any prohibition on using social media for speech protected by the National Labor Relations Act, such as candidly discussing wages, hours and working conditions.

The tension is clear: Social networks encourage fast, constant, brief communications; journalism calls for communication preceded by fact-finding and thoughtful consideration. Journalism has many "unsend" buttons, including editors. Social networks have none. Everything we say online can be used against us in a court of law, in the minds of subjects and sources and by people who for reasons of their own may want to cast us in a negative light. While, obviously, we cannot control what others may post on our accounts, we must maintain constant awareness when posting to Facebook, Twitter and other online fora that we are flying without a net, and that an indiscretion lasts forever. At all costs, we must avoid flame wars, incendiary rhetoric and loose talk. We should also remember that by friending or following someone, we may be giving out the identity of a source. Everything depends on our keeping trust.

In other words, be careful. By all means, explore ways in which social media can help you do your job. But before you tweet or post, consider how what you're doing will reflect on your professionalism and our collective reputation. When in doubt, talk to colleagues, your editor or your supervisor.

ID Theft Policy of a Bank

Safeguarding Consumer Information

xxxxx Bank maintains internal controls sufficient to protect customer financial information as outlined in our Information Security Policy and procedures.

The Bank's Information Security Program is designed to:

- Ensure the security and confidentiality of our customer's information;
- Protect against any anticipated threats or hazards to the security or integrity of such information;
- Protect against unauthorized access to or use of such information that could result in substantial harm or inconvenience to any customer; and
- Ensure the proper disposal of customer information and consumer information.

Incident Response Handling Program

The Bank maintains a process for internal reporting of suspicious or fraudulent activity, including identity theft. If sensitive personal information is compromised, we will follow the procedures outlined in our Incident Response Handling Program and procedures.

The Bank's Incident Response Handling Program is designed to:

- Assess the nature and scope of an incident, and identify what customer information systems and types of customer information has been accessed or misused;
- Notify the FDIC as soon as possible when the Bank becomes aware of an incident involving sensitive customer information;
- Notify appropriate law enforcement authorities, in addition, to filing a timely incident reports in situations involving federal criminal violations requiring immediate attention;
- Take appropriate steps to contain and control the incident to prevent further unauthorized access or use of customer information; and
- Notify customers when warranted.

If you think that your identity may have been compromised please follow the recommended steps provided in **The Federal Trade Commissions (FTC) website**.

Source: [9]

Technical Requirements for a Bank's Website

To provide you the most effective and secure online access to xxxxx Bank accounts and services, we strongly recommend that you use or upgrade to the latest version of software supported by xxxx Bank. If you have any questions, please **contact us**.

Browser Requirements

We are continually upgrading our online services to provide you with the most valuable and secure online access. As we add new features and enhancements to our service, there are certain browser versions and operating systems that do not support these changes.

The current supported browsers are:

- Internet Explorer 9.0 or later; Mozilla Firefox (Current Version)
- Google Chrome (Current Version); Apple Safari 6.0 or later

PDF Requirements

Adobe Reader (Version 11.0 or later) is required to access documents being provided to you in PDF format (for example, Online Statements or Spending Reports). Click on Adobe System Requirements to determine the latest requirements. The basic **Adobe Reader software** is available for free directly from **Adobe**.

Important PDF Reminder

For Mac users

If you access a PDF document from a Mac, the PDF may be automatically copied to its desktop or to an easily accessible download folder.

For PC users

If you access a PDF document from a PC the PDF may remain among its cached files.

Personal information may easily be accessed by others using the same computer if left on the desktop, in a download folder or in the cache. If you are in a non-secure location, be sure to delete the file after viewing it and empty the Trash (for Macs) and or clear your cache (for PCs).

Hardware and Operating System Requirements

Please consult with your browser vendor and Adobe to obtain the minimum hardware and operating system requirements that apply to the software versions you are currently using or wish to install.

The current minimum OS versions are:

- Windows Vista or later
- Mac OS 10.7 or later

Please Note:

When you make changes to your computer software or equipment, our system may require you to re-confirm your identity online the next time you visit our web site to conduct online transactions. This is for your own protection.

Source: [9]

Code of Conduct for a Financial Institution

Do the right thing — the importance of the Code
Our values and our brand promise are integral to the way we work every day. The Code is important because it outlines how we can make sure that the decisions we make are the right ones.

Act responsibly and within authority
Be disciplined, responsible and take accountability for the risks you take and make sure they are appropriate to your business or activity. You must keep to our limits and policies and not make decisions that are beyond your delegated authority.

Use good judgment
Recognise when there are situations without simple solutions. Use the Code's decision making framework to help you make decisions well, appropriately and with care.

Speaking Up
You have a responsibility to Speak Up when you see behaviour, a process or system you are not comfortable with at work. This helps to maintain a culture of strong ethics, integrity and transparency.

Comply with laws, regulations and Group standards
You are individually responsible for complying with the spirit, not just the letter, of laws, regulations and our Group standards.

Combat financial crime
It is critically important to protect the worldwide financial system. You must comply with laws, regulations and Group standards on anti-money laundering (including those on tax evasion), preventing financing for terrorism, fraud or sanctions.

Reject bribery and corruption
Bribery is illegal, dishonest and damages the communities where it takes place. You must not give or accept bribes nor take part in any form of corruption.

Treat clients fairly
A focus on building long-term relationships helps to increase our business by improving our reputation. This includes having well-designed products and services, which:
- Are clearly sold based on suitable advice
- Perform as expected
- Give clients choice

Manage conflicts of interest

It is important not to put yourself in a position where your judgment could be affected. You are responsible for identifying, assessing and managing conflicts of interest (whether actual or issues which could be viewed as conflicts) that arise in your daily working life.

Do not engage in or support insider dealing

The misuse of inside information undermines the financial system and unfairly disadvantages others in the market. You must keep to the Group Personal Account Dealing Policy to deal with the risk of insider dealing.

Protect confidential information

Building trust is a basic part of all our relationships with clients. You must not release confidential information unless authorised to do so.

Compete fairly in the market place

You must understand and comply with the laws which affect how you compete in your markets both locally and abroad.

Treat colleagues fairly and with respect

All staff are entitled to a safe working environment that is inclusive and free from discrimination, bullying and harassment. Treating your colleagues as partners helps our people to deliver on the brand promise, resulting in a positive effect on our business results.

Be open and co-operate with regulators

Deal with regulators in a responsive, open and co-operative way and give regulators information they would reasonably expect to be told about.

Respect our communities and the environment

To contribute to economic stability in our markets, we all have a responsibility to reduce our effect on the environment and give back to our communities.

Source: [9]

Bring Your Own Device

IT Manager Daily (http://www.itmanagerdaily.com/byod-policy-template/) published this basic template by Megan Berry. According to Megan,

> "Bring your own device (BYOD) programs call for three critical components: a software application for managing the devices connecting to the network, a written policy outlining the responsibilities of both the employer and the users, and an agreement users must sign, acknowledging that they have read and understand the policy." [13]

A BYOD policy forces firms to consider the appropriate and acceptable use of personal computing devices such as smartphones and tablets on the firm's network. Common questions include: Which devices (in terms of standards and specifications) may be acceptable on the firm's network? Which web browsers should employees use? Which security tools are appropriate for acceptable devices? What level of support is IT department expected to provide? To make it comprehensive, BYOD should get input from all functions of the organization including HR, IT, accounting, and executives alike.

Below is a template shared by Megan in her IT Manager Daily blog [13].

Company XYZ: BYOD Policy

Company XYZ grants its employees the privilege of purchasing and using smartphones and tablets of their choosing at work for their convenience. Company XYZ reserves the right to revoke this privilege if users do not abide by the policies and procedures outlined below.

This policy is intended to protect the security and integrity of Company XYZ's data and technology infrastructure. Limited exceptions to the policy may occur due to variations in devices and platforms.

XYZ employees must agree to the terms and conditions set forth in this policy in order to be able to connect their devices to the company network.

Acceptable Use
- The company defines acceptable business use as activities that directly or indirectly support the business of Company XYZ.
- The company defines acceptable personal use on company time as reasonable and limited personal communication or recreation, such as reading or game playing.
- Employees are blocked from accessing certain websites during work hours/while connected to the corporate network at the discretion of the company. Such websites include, but are not limited to youtube.com, and facebook.com
- Devices' camera and/or video capabilities are/are not disabled while on-site.
- Devices may not be used at any time to:
    - Store or transmit illicit materials
    - Store or transmit proprietary information belonging to another company

- - Harass others
  - Engage in outside business activities
  - Etc.
- The following apps are allowed: (include a detailed list of apps, such as weather, productivity apps, Facebook, etc., which will be permitted)
- The following apps are not allowed: (apps not downloaded through iTunes or Google Play, etc.)
- Employees may use their mobile device to access the following company-owned resources: email, calendars, contacts, documents, etc.
- Company XYZ has a zero-tolerance policy for texting or emailing while driving and only hands-free talking while driving is permitted.

Devices and Support
- Smartphones including iPhone, Android, Blackberry and Windows phones are allowed (the list should be as detailed as necessary including models, operating systems, versions, etc.).
- Tablets including iPad and Android are allowed (the list should be as detailed as necessary including models, operating systems, versions, etc.).
- Connectivity issues are supported by IT; employees should/should not contact the device manufacturer or their carrier for operating system or hardware-related issues.
- Devices must be presented to IT for proper job provisioning and configuration of standard apps, such as browsers, office productivity software and security tools, before they can access the network.

Reimbursement
- The company will/will not reimburse the employee for a percentage of the cost of the device (include the amount of the company's contribution), or The company will contribute X amount of money toward the cost of the device.
- The company will a) pay the employee an allowance, b) cover the cost of the entire phone/data plan, c) pay half of the phone/data plan, etc.
- The company will/will not reimburse the employee for the following charges: roaming, plan overages, etc.

Security
- In order to prevent unauthorized access, devices must be password protected using the features of the device and a strong password is required to access the company network.
- The company's strong password policy is: Passwords must be at least six characters and a combination of upper- and lower-case letters, numbers and symbols. Passwords will be rotated every 90 days and the new password can't be one of 15 previous passwords.
- The device must lock itself with a password or PIN if it's idle for five minutes.
- After five failed login attempts, the device will lock. Contact IT to regain access.
- Rooted (Android) or jailbroken (iOS) devices are strictly forbidden from accessing the network.
- Employees are automatically prevented from downloading, installing and using any app that does not appear on the company's list of approved apps.
- Smartphones and tablets that are not on the company's list of supported devices are/are not allowed to connect to the network. Devices belonging to employees that are for

personal use only are/are not allowed to connect to the network.

- Employees' access to company data is limited based on user profiles defined by IT and automatically enforced.
- The employee's device may be remotely wiped if 1) the device is lost, 2) the employee terminates his or her employment, 3) IT detects a data or policy breach, a virus or similar threat to the security of the company's data and technology infrastructure.

Risks/Liabilities/Disclaimers

- While IT will take every precaution to prevent the employee's personal data from being lost in the event it must remote wipe a device, it is the employee's responsibility to take additional precautions, such as backing up email, and contacts.
- The company reserves the right to disconnect devices or disable services without notification.
- Lost or stolen devices must be reported to the company within 24 hours. Employees are responsible for notifying their mobile carrier immediately upon loss of a device.
- The employee is expected to use his or her devices in an ethical manner at all times and adhere to the company's acceptable use policy as outlined above.
- The employee is personally liable for all costs associated with his or her device.
- The employee assumes full liability for risks including, but not limited to, the partial or complete loss of company and personal data due to an operating system crash, errors, bugs, viruses, malware, and/or other software or hardware failures, or programming errors that render the device unusable.
- Company XYZ reserves the right to take appropriate disciplinary action up to and including termination for noncompliance with this policy.

Source: [13]

Acceptable Use Policy

The following document is a sample Acceptable Use Security Policy using the outline identified in the Security Policy Template [14].

OT Company Policy

INFORMATION SECURITY

NUMBER: 29244
EFFECTIVE DATE: 03/04/2014

REVISED DATE: 26/08/2016

SUBJECT: ACCEPTABLE USE POLICY   STATUS: APPROVED

Section 1 - Introduction

Information Resources are strategic assets of the OT Company and must be treated and managed as valuable resources. OT Company provides various computer resources to its employees for the purpose of assisting them in the performance of their job-related duties. State law permits incidental access to state resources for personal use. This policy clearly documents expectations for appropriate use of OT Company assets. This Acceptable Use Policy in conjunction with the corresponding standards is established to achieve the following:

1. To establish appropriate and acceptable practices regarding the use of information resources.
2. To ensure compliance with applicable State law and other rules and regulations regarding the management of information resources.
3. To educate individuals who may use information resources with respect to their responsibilities associated with computer resource use.

This Acceptable Use Policy contains four policy directives.   Part I – Acceptable Use Management, Part II – Ownership, Part III – Acceptable Use, and Part IV – Incidental Use. Together, these directives form the foundation of the OT Company Acceptable Use Program.

Section 2 – Roles & Responsibilities

1. OT Company management will establish a periodic reporting requirement to measure the compliance and effectiveness of this policy.
2. OT Company management is responsible for implementing the requirements of this policy, or documenting non-compliance via the method described under exception handling.
3. OT Company Managers, in cooperation with Security Management Division, are required to train employees on policy and document issues with Policy compliance.
4. All OT Company employees are required to read and acknowledge the reading of this policy.

Section 3 – Policy Directives
Part I Acceptable Use Management Requirements

1. OT Company will establish formal Standards and Processes to support the ongoing development and maintenance of the OT Company Acceptable Use Policy.
2. The OT Company Director and Management will commit to the ongoing training and education of OT Companye staff responsible for the administration and/or maintenance and/or use of OT Company Information Resources. At a minimum, skills to be included or advanced include User Training and Awareness
3. The OT Company Director and Management will use metrics to establish the need for additional education or awareness program in order to facilitate the reduction in the threat and vulnerability profiles of OT Company Assets and Information Resources.
4. The OT Company Director and Managers will establish a formal review cycle for all Acceptable Use initiatives.
5. Any security issues discovered will be reported to the CISO or his designee for follow-up investigation. Additional Reporting requirements can be located within the Policy Enforcement, Auditing and Reporting section of this policy.

Part II - Ownership

Electronic files created, sent, received, or stored on Information Resources owned, leased, administered, or otherwise under the custody and control of OT Company are the property of OT Company and employee use of these such files is neither personal nor private. Authorized OT Company Information Security employees may access all such files at any time without knowledge of the Information Resources user or owner. OT Company management reserves the right to monitor and/or log all employee use of OT Company Information Resources with or without prior notice.

Part III – Acceptable Use Requirements

1. Users must report any weaknesses in OT Company computer security to the appropriate security staff. Weaknesses in computer security include unexpected software or system behavior, which may result in unintentional disclosure of information or exposure to security threats.
2. Users must report any incidents of possible misuse or violation of this Acceptable Use Policy through the use of documented Misuse Reporting processes associated with the Internet, Intranet, and Email use standards.
3. Users must not attempt to access any data, documents, email correspondence, and programs contained on OT Company systems for which they do not have authorization.
4. Systems administrators and authorized users must not divulge remote connection modem phone numbers or other access points to OT Company computer resources to anyone without proper authorization.
5. Users must not share their account(s), passwords, Personal Identification Numbers (PIN), Security Tokens (i.e. Smartcard), or similar information or devices used for identification and authorization purposes.
6. Users must not make unauthorized copies of copyrighted or OT Company owned software.
7. Users must not use non-standard shareware or freeware software without the appropriate OT Company Management approval.

8. Users must not purposely engage in activity that may harass, threaten or abuse others or intentionally access, create, store or transmit material which OT Company may deem to be offensive, indecent or obscene, or that is illegal according to local, state or federal law.

9. Users must not engage in activity that may degrade the performance of Information Resources; deprive an authorized user access to OT Company resources; obtain extra resources beyond those allocated; or circumvent OT Company computer security measures.

10. Users must not download, install or run security programs or utilities such as password cracking programs, packet sniffers, or port scanners that reveal or exploit weaknesses in the security of a OT Company computer resource unless approved by OT Company's Chief Information Security Officer (CISO).

11. OT Company Information Resources must not be used for personal benefit, political activity, unsolicited advertising, unauthorized fund raising, or for the solicitation of performance of any activity that is prohibited by any local, state or federal law.

12. Access to the Internet from OT Company owned, home based, computers must adhere to all the policies. Employees must not allow family members or other non-employees to access nonpublic accessible OT Company computer systems.

13. Any security issues discovered will be reported to the CISO or his designee for follow-up investigation. Additional Reporting requirements can be located within the Policy Enforcement, Auditing and Reporting section of this policy.

Part IV – Incidental Use

Government Code Section 8314 permits incidental personal use of state resources. At OT Company this means:

1. Incidental personal use of electronic mail, Internet access, fax machines, printers, and copiers is restricted to OT Company approved users only and does not include family members or others not affiliated with OT Company.

2. Incidental use must not result in direct costs to OT Company, cause legal action against, or cause embarrassment to OT Company

3. Incidental use must not interfere with the normal performance of an employee's work duties.

4. Storage of personal email messages, voice messages, files and documents within OT Company's computer resources must be nominal.

OT Company management will resolve incidental use questions and issues using these guidelines in collaboration with OT Company's CISO, HR Manager and Chief Counsel.

Section 4 - Enforcement, Auditing, Reporting

1. Violation of this policy may result in disciplinary action that may include termination for employees and temporaries; termination of employment relations in the case of contractors or consultants; dismissal for interns and volunteers. Additionally, individuals are subject to loss of OT Company Information Resources access privileges, civil, and criminal prosecution. *(Note: Agencies need to be aware of the constantly changing legal framework of the environment in which they operate, and they must adapt accordingly. Appropriate legal advisors and/or human resources representatives should review the policy and all of the procedures in use for policy enforcement. Some legal/human*

resources believe it is not necessary to include this section because all policy is enforceable. In fact, if it is included in one, it may be detrimental to the enforcement of other policies that do not include the section.)

2. OT Company Management is responsible for the periodic auditing and reporting of compliance with this policy. OT Company Executives will be responsible for defining the format and frequency of the reporting requirements and communicating those requirements, in writing, to OT Company Management.

3. Exceptions to this policy will be considered only when the requested exception is documented using the Exception Handling Process and Form and submitted to the OT Company Chief Information Security Officer and OT Company Policy Review Committee.

4. Any employee may, at any time, anonymously report policy violations via OT Company's Intranet or by telephone at 444-35456.

Section 5 - References

Government Code Section 8314
8314.5 - Internet Use Standard
8314.6 - Internet Content Filtering
8314.7 - E-Mail Use Standard
8314.8 - Intranet use Standard

Section 6 - Control and Maintenance

Policy Version: 29244
Date: 26/08/2016
Author: Tawiah Asem
Owner: OT Company Chief Information Security Officer

OT Company Policy will be reviewed and revised in accordance with parameters established in the Information Security Charter and Policy Management Process.

Network Connection Policy

Brown University has a university-wide network connection policy to define the standards for connecting to computers, networks and servers in the University [15]. The policy detailed below.

Brown University's Network Connection Policy

1.0 Purpose

This policy is designed to protect the campus network and the ability of members of the Brown community to use it. The purpose of this policy is to define the standards for connecting computers, servers or other devices to the University's network. The standards are designed to minimize the potential exposure to Brown University and our community from damages (including financial, loss of work, and loss of data) that could result from computers and servers that are not configured or maintained properly and to ensure that devices on the network are not taking actions that could adversely affect network performance.

Brown University must provide a secure network for our educational, research, instructional and administrative needs and services. An unsecured computer on the network allows denial of service attacks, viruses, Trojans, and other compromises to enter the university's campus network, thereby affecting many computers, as well as the network's integrity. Damages from these exploits could include the loss of sensitive and confidential data, interruption of network services and damage to critical Brown University internal systems. Universities that have experienced severe compromises have also experienced damage to their public image. Therefore, individuals who connect computers, servers and other devices to the Brown network must follow specific standards and take specific actions.

2.0 Scope

This policy applies to all members of the Brown University community or visitors who have any device connected to the Brown University network, including, but not limited to, desktop computers, laptops, servers, wireless computers, mobile devices, smartphones, specialized equipment, cameras, environmental control systems, and telephone system components. The policy also applies to anyone who has systems outside the campus network that access the campus network and resources. The policy applies to university-owned computers (including those purchased with grant funds), personally-owned or leased computers that connect to the Brown network.

3.0 Policy

3.1 Appropriate Connection Methods

You may connect devices to the campus network at appropriate connectivity points including voice/data jacks, through an approved wireless network access point, via a VPN or SSH tunnel, or through remote access mechanisms such as DSL, cable modems, and traditional modems over phone lines.

Modifications or extensions to the network can frequently cause undesired effects, including loss of connectivity. These effects are not always immediate, nor are they always located at the site of modifications. As a result, extending or modifying the Brown network must be done within the CIS published guidelines. Exceptions will be made by CIS for approved personnel in departments who can demonstrate competence with managing the aforementioned hardware.

3.2 Network Registration

Users of the university network may be required to authenticate when connecting a device to it. Users may also need to install an agent on their computers before they are allowed on the network. The role of such an agent would be to audit the computer for compliance with security standards as defined in section 3.4 below.

CIS maintains a database of unique machine identification, network address and owner for the purposes of contacting the owner of a computer when it is necessary. For example, CIS would contact the registered owner of a computer when his or her computer has been compromised and is launching a denial of service attack or if a copyright violation notice has been issued for the IP address used by that person.

3.3 Responsibility for Security

Every computer or other device connected to the network, including a desktop computer has an associated owner (e.g. a student who has a personal computer) or caretaker (e.g. a staff member who has a computer in her office). For the sake of this policy, owners and caretakers are both referred to as owners.

Owners are responsible for ensuring that their machines meet the relevant security standards and for managing the security of the equipment and the services that run on it. Some departments may assign the responsibility for computer security and maintenance to the Departmental Computing Coordinator or the Departmental Systems Administrator. Therefore, it is possible that one owner manages multiple departmental machines plus his or her own personal computer. Every owner should know who is responsible for maintaining his or her machine(s).

3.4 Security Standards

These security standards apply to all devices that connect to the Brown University network through standard university ports, through wireless services, and through home and off campus connections.

- Owners must ensure that all computers and other devices capable of running anti-virus/anti-malware software have Brown-licensed anti-virus software (or other appropriate virus protection products) installed and running. Owners should update definition files at least once per week. See CIS's Software Catalog for more information.

- Computer owners must install the most recent security patches on the system as soon as practical or as directed by Information Security. Where machines cannot be patched, other actions may need to be taken to secure the machine appropriately.

- Computer owners of computers that contain Brown Restricted Information should apply extra protections. CIS's Information Security Group will provide consultations on request to computer owners who would like more information on further security measures. For instance, individuals who are maintaining files with Social Security information or other sensitive personal information should take extra care in managing their equipment and securing it appropriately.

3.5 Centrally-Provided Network-Based Services

CIS, the central computing organization, is responsible for providing reliable network services for the entire campus. As such, individuals or departments may not run any service which disrupts or interferes with centrally-provided services. These services include, but are not limited to, email, DNS, DHCP, and Domain Registration. Exceptions will be made by CIS for approved personnel in departments who can demonstrate competence with managing the aforementioned services. Also, individuals or departments may not run any service or server which requests from an individual their CIS-maintained password.

3.6 Protection of the Network

CIS uses multiple methods to protect the Brown network:

- monitoring for external intruders

- scanning hosts on the network for suspicious anomalies

- blocking harmful traffic

All network traffic passing in or out of Brown's network is monitored by an intrusion detection system for signs of compromises. By connecting a computer or device to the network, you are acknowledging that the network traffic to and from your computer may be scanned.

CIS routinely scans the Brown network, looking for vulnerabilities. At times, more extensive testing may be necessary to detect and confirm the existence of vulnerabilities. By connecting to the network, you agree to have your computer or device scanned for possible vulnerabilities.

CIS reserves the right to take necessary steps to contain security exposures to the University and or improper network traffic. CIS will take action to contain devices that exhibit the behaviors indicated below, and allow normal traffic and central services to resume.

- imposing an exceptional load on a campus service

- exhibiting a pattern of network traffic that disrupts centrally provided services

- exhibiting a pattern of malicious network traffic associated with scanning or attacking others

- exhibiting behavior consistent with host compromise

CIS reserves the right to restrict certain types of traffic coming into and across the Brown network. CIS restricts traffic that is known to cause damage to the network or hosts on it, such as NETBIOS. CIS also may control other types of traffic that consume too much network capacity, such as file-sharing traffic.

By connecting to the network, you acknowledge that a computer or device that exhibits any of the behaviors listed above is in violation of this policy and will be removed from the network until it meets compliancy standards.

4.0 Related Policies and Links

Acceptable Use
Policy on the Handling of Brown Restricted Information
Guidelines for Extension of Network Services

Questions or comments to: ITPolicy@brown.edu

Effective Date: March 19, 2004
Last Reviewed: January, 2015
Next Scheduled Review: January, 2017

Web Publishing Guidelines

These guidelines constitute what is expected in posting and managing content on an organizational website. We will explore an example from The Institute of Education Sciences (IES), the statistics, research, and evaluation arm of the U.S. Department of Education [21].

Web Publishing Guidelines
Forum Unified Education Technology Institute [21]

Introduction

Because basic websites are not difficult to develop, many schools and individual students are creating their own Internet sites. Any site associated with an education organization will reflect on that organization, so it is important to develop policies that ensure consistency, while not stifling creativity. This appendix discusses guidelines an organization should consider to present a functional site that reflects its mission. Guidelines address establishment of a content approval process, determining a site's "look and feel," and control of updates and revisions.

Guidelines that incorporate procedures and regulations in the areas of content, technology, and usability are effective in developing a foundation to maintain an effective, user-friendly, and secure site. Education organizations need to be aware of privacy rights, factors that affect how webpages are displayed by different browsers, and especially the many security issues related to Internet and web access in schools and education organizations. Organization guidelines should be made available to all people (i.e., staff members, contractors, volunteers, and students) who develop or post content to the site.

Because any website associated with an education organization will reflect on the organization, it is important to develop policies that will ensure appropriate content and consistent presentation without stifling the creativity of students, staff members, and other contributors.

Content Guidelines

Many times, the first impression the public has of an education organization is its website. In addition to reflecting the organization's mission and containing appropriate and useful content, the site should be attractive and well organized. A district, for example, may decide to include a page on its website about employment opportunities. If the application procedures on the site enhance the ease of applying and contain useful information about employment in the district, the site may help the district attract new teachers. A disorganized website will likely create a poor impression of the district and may turn prospective teachers away.

Regardless of the sophistication of the site, several basic management rules apply. First, the site should be organized so that a novice can navigate easily from one section to the next. A good rule for all but the most complicated sites is that the user should be no more than two "clicks" (i.e., links) away from important information. Links to sites that are outside the control of the organization should be clearly identified. Second, pages should be neat, clean, and clear—a cluttered screen makes it difficult to find the content. Finally, each page should be checked periodically to ensure that all graphics are loading properly and that all links are active. If the organization does not have the resources to support a sophisticated site, it is better to start with a simple site that can be kept current and operational than to have a site filled with "under construction" graphics and/or outdated information.

Links to sites that are outside the control of the organization should be identified by clear and explicit warnings. For example:
You are now leaving the [insert name of organization] website. We have provided a link to this site because it has information that may be of interest to our users; however, [insert name of organization] does not necessarily endorse the views expressed or the information presented on this external site.

In many cases, education organizations perceive the website primarily as a vehicle for informing staff, students, and the general public about their activities and goals. To effectively administer content on the organization's website, policy and procedural guidelines should be established as a component of the organization's technology plan before proceeding with website development.

Guidelines for Posting New Content
The first step, before any programming begins, is to determine what the organization needs and wants the website to do. Beautiful sites can be created with flashing icons, dynamic colors, and interesting text. However, if the content does not meet the needs of the organization, the value is, at best, limited. Everyone has visited a website that is difficult to navigate—where one has to spend a great deal of time "clicking" around the site, or where links to other sites do not work. Without guidelines and a quality control process, problems like these are inevitable.

The organization should develop a clear process for deciding what and how new materials are posted to the website, including whether an approval procedure is needed for new sites and pages. The procedure may be as simple as a request for space on the organization's server, or it may be a more complex process involving a formal review of proposed sites and pages prior to approval. It is important for the organization to distribute the guidelines for posting new content and to make sure that staff members are aware of the process. Posting the procedures and content guidelines on the website for easy access can accomplish this task. Additionally, it is imperative that staff members understand the procedures and guidelines.

Local coordinators and students may develop innovative school websites in-house. While the organization will want to support such innovation, the use of nonprofessional web developers makes strong guidelines even more important. Because the district is ultimately responsible for the content on school websites, it may be in the district's best interest to have a representative (e.g., a school site coordinator or webmaster) at each school who understands and is able to support and enforce district guidelines and regulations.

When the district is unable to assign a site coordinator or webmaster, every effort should be made to ensure that there is a person familiar with district guidelines and other regulations at every location where someone has posting authority.

What Should the Content on a Website Look Like?

Website design should present a consistent look and feel for a sense of continuity across a site's pages. One way to accomplish this is through the use of style sheets that are embedded or linked to the site within the programming design. Style sheets, or templates, define the format for each page in terms of elements such as type face, margin width, heading specifications, spacing, and layout.

This does not mean that all pages need to look the same. Not all webpages on a site will use style sheets. The purpose of style sheets and other formatting tools or guides is to create consistency, not stifle creativity. However, each style sheet should contain:

- a home button that returns the user to the site's home page with one click of the mouse
- the name, address, and telephone number of the organization
- the webmaster's e-mail address
- copyright notification
- a privacy statement

Advertising on the Website

The organization must address the issue of advertising on its website. Product advertising is allowed in some schools and districts or at some venues within a school or district (e.g., at athletic events). Other organizations do not permit advertising under any circumstances. Policy decisions regarding website advertising should be consistent with other organizational policies concerning advertising. Organizations should be wary of Internet Service Providers (ISPs) that offer "free" disk space or other services in exchange for the right to display advertising on the site. Some of these services will run banner advertisements or pop-up ads while the user (in the school's case, a student) is online. Some ISPs even profile users, then sell their names and other access information to other service providers or advertisers. While this process is commonplace on the Internet, it may be inappropriate for school or district sites.

Some organizations have determined that it is in the best interest of the students and staff to limit website access to government and other research sites that do not carry commercial endorsements or permit "pop-up" advertising. This is accomplished by using a program to filter out unwanted sites. Situations also exist in which a vendor who programs a website or a donor who funds a website requests that the organization place an "icon" on its home page to advertise their contribution. If the organization agrees to place an icon of this type on the website, many more requests may follow.

Website Disclaimer

A disclaimer statement should appear on the organization's website to acknowledge that the public is free to browse the site. The statement should include information about copyrighted material and may include language that disclaims responsibility for some Internet activities. The organization should consult with legal counsel about the specific language and content of the disclaimer. To view an example of a website disclaimer, visit West Virginia's State Department of Education website.

Technical Guidelines

There are several technical guidelines the organization should employ when webpages are created. If the organization's website is to be maintained and updated by more than one person, an established set of procedures for accomplishing these tasks will help to ensure dependability and consistency. The technical guidelines developed by the organization can serve as the procedural handbook for implementing policies governing web use. Aspects to consider when developing technical guidelines include:

- compatibility of guidelines with recent releases of the major web browsers, as well as with older browsers
- optimization for different web browsers
- load time of the website using a variety of connection speeds
- use of approved file extensions and directory structure
- use of an Internet-friendly color palette
- content of meta tags—information inserted into the "head area" of the webpage—to improve access to the organization's website by search engines from outside the organization
- removal of unnecessary HTML tags
- use of standard navigation bars and icons throughout the site
- determination of whether to use, or prohibit, frames

Contractors who develop sites for educational organizations should be subject to the same guidelines concerning website development as are in-house developers. While a contractor may have access to additional technical standards and guidelines, the organization is still responsible for content, accessibility, and style. Accordingly, there should be clear standards and procedures in place when the contractor is selected, and the contractor should agree to abide by all of the standards before the organization signs a contract.

Password Security

The use of passwords is important for securing the privacy and confidentiality of student and personnel information. Passwords can also assist the organization in monitoring access to mission-critical applications. All organizations that maintain a website, including schools, should consider policy issues related to password security. These procedures should be written and distributed to all members of the organization. Relevant password issues include the following:

- A password should consist of both alphabetic and numeric characters.
- The organization should require that passwords be of a sufficient length (e.g., at least eight characters).
- The organization should establish procedures that require passwords to be changed frequently (e.g., every 30 to 60 days).
- Passwords should not be shared or "loaned" to another person.
- Passwords should not be written down.

Password-related security procedures might include the establishment of a help desk or an automated process for staff members to contact when a password is forgotten. Password restoration procedures should include a method for verifying the identity of the person calling the help desk. This could include recalling the staff member's social security number, mother's maiden name, place of birth, or other item that will identify the person requesting a new password.

Summary
1. Organizations should establish guidelines for posting content on a website.
2. Website content guidelines should address consistency without stifling creativity.
3. Organizations should develop procedures to deal with advertising on the Internet, especially if the organization uses an outside ISP to host the website.
4. Technical guidelines are necessary for password protection.

Employee Information and Technology Security Agreement

This sample is shared by The Institute of Education Sciences [22]. An organization can refer to this sample as it develops its own Information and Technology Security Agreements for staff, contractors, and other individuals who are to be given access to equipment, information, or networks.

Employee Information and Technology Security Agreement
I acknowledge that [name of organization]'s information and technology security policies, guidelines, and procedures have been made available to me for review and consideration. I also certify that I have been given ample opportunity to have any and all questions about my responsibilities addressed. I am, therefore, aware that I am accountable for information and technology security procedures as they govern the acceptable performance of my job. I understand that failure to abide by any and all policies, guidelines, and procedures can result in organizational, civil, or criminal action and/or the termination of my employment.

Signature: _____ Printed Name: _____

Job Title: _____ Date:

_____/_____/_____Contractor/Consultant/Outsider Information and Technology Security Agreement

I acknowledge that [name of organization] has provided me with adequate time to review and consider the information and technology security policies, guidelines, and procedures it deems applicable to responsibilities I am undertaking on behalf of [name of organization], regardless of my employment status. I also certify that I have been given ample opportunity to have any and all questions about my responsibilities addressed. I am, therefore, aware that I am accountable for those information and technology security procedures as they relate to my work for, or on the behalf of, [name of organization]. I understand that failure to abide by any and all policies, guidelines, and procedures can result in organizational, civil, or criminal action and/or the termination of my relationship with [name of organization].

Signature: _____ Printed Name: _____

Job Title: _____ Date: _____/_____/_____

Data Breach Response Policy

Data Breach Response policy defines the goals and the vision for the breach response process. This policy defines to whom it applies and under what circumstances, and it will include the definition of a breach, staff roles and responsibilities, standards and metrics (e.g., to enable prioritization of the incidents), as well as reporting, remediation, and feedback mechanisms. This sample is shared by SANS Security Policy Resource page [23].

1.0 Purpose

The purpose of the policy is to establish the goals and the vision for the breach response process. This policy will clearly define to whom it applies and under what circumstances, and it will include the definition of a breach, staff roles and responsibilities, standards and metrics (e.g., to enable prioritization of the incidents), as well as reporting, remediation, and feedback mechanisms. The policy shall be well publicized and made easily available to all personnel whose duties involve data privacy and security protection.

OT Company Information Security's intentions for publishing a Data Breach Response Policy are to focus significant attention on data security and data security breaches and how OT Company's established culture of openness, trust and integrity should respond to such activity. OT Company Information Security is committed to protecting OT Company's employees, partners and the company from illegal or damaging actions by individuals, either knowingly or unknowingly.

1.1 Background

This policy mandates that any individual who suspects that a theft, breach or exposure of OT Company Protected data or OT Company Sensitive data has occurred must immediately provide a description of what occurred via e-mail to Helpdesk@OT Company.org, by calling 555-1212, or through the use of the help desk reporting web page at http://OT Company. This e-mail address, phone number, and web page are monitored by the OT Company's Information Security Administrator. This team will investigate all reported thefts, data breaches and exposures to confirm if a theft, breach or exposure has occurred. If a theft, breach or exposure has occurred, the Information Security Administrator will follow the appropriate procedure in place.

2.0 Scope

This policy applies to all whom collect, access, maintain, distribute, process, protect, store, use, transmit, dispose of, or otherwise handle personally identifiable information or Protected Health Information (PHI) of OT Company members. Any agreements with vendors will contain language similar that protects the fund.

3.0 Policy Confirmed theft, data breach or exposure of OT Company Protected data or OT Company Sensitive data

As soon as a theft, data breach or exposure containing OT Company Protected data or OT Company Sensitive data is identified, the process of removing all access to that resource will begin.

The Executive Director will chair an incident response team to handle the breach or exposure.

The team will include members from:
- IT Infrastructure
- IT Applications
- Finance (if applicable)
- Legal
- Communications
- Member Services (if Member data is affected)
- Human Resources
- The affected unit or department that uses the involved system or output or whose data may have been breached or exposed
- Additional departments based on the data type involved, Additional individuals as deemed necessary by the Executive Director

Confirmed theft, breach or exposure of OT Company data

The Executive Director will be notified of the theft, breach or exposure. IT, along with the designated forensic team, will analyze the breach or exposure to determine the root cause.

Work with Forensic Investigators

As provided by OT Company cyber insurance, the insurer will need to provide access to forensic investigators and experts that will determine how the breach or exposure occurred; the types of data involved; the number of internal/external individuals and/or organizations impacted; and analyze the breach or exposure to determine the root cause.

Develop a communication plan.

Work with OT Company communications, legal and human resource departments to decide how to communicate the breach to: a) internal employees, b) the public, and c) those directly affected.

3.2 Ownership and Responsibilities

- Sponsors - Sponsors are those members of the OT Company community that have primary responsibility for maintaining any particular information resource. Sponsors may be designated by any OT Company Executive in connection with their administrative responsibilities, or by the actual sponsorship, collection, development, or storage of information.

- Information Security Administrator is that member of the OT Company community, designated by the Executive Director or the Director, Information Technology (IT) Infrastructure, who provides administrative support for the implementation, oversight and coordination of security procedures and systems with respect to specific information resources in consultation with the relevant Sponsors.
- Users include virtually all members of the OT Company community to the extent they have authorized access to information resources, and may include staff, trustees, contractors, consultants, interns, temporary employees and volunteers.
- The Incident Response Team shall be chaired by Executive Management and shall include, but will not be limited to, the following departments or their representatives: IT-Infrastructure, IT-Application Security; Communications; Legal; Management; Financial Services, Member Services; Human Resources.

4.0 Enforcement

Any OT Company personnel found in violation of this policy may be subject to disciplinary action, up to and including termination of employment. Any third party partner company found in violation may have their network connection terminated.

5.0 Definitions

Encryption or encrypted data – The most effective way to achieve data security. To read an encrypted file, you must have access to a secret key or password that enables you to decrypt it. Unencrypted data is called plain text;

Plain text – Unencrypted data.

Hacker – A slang term for a computer enthusiast, i.e., a person who enjoys learning programming languages and computer systems and can often be considered an expert on the subject(s).

Protected Health Information (PHI) - Under US law is any information about health status, provision of health care, or payment for health care that is created or collected by a "Covered Entity" (or a Business Associate of a Covered Entity), and can be linked to a specific individual.

Personally Identifiable Information (PII) - Any data that could potentially identify a specific individual. Any information that can be used to distinguish one person from another and can be used for de-anonymizing anonymous data can be considered

Protected data - See PII and PHI

Information Resource - The data and information assets of an organization, department or unit.

Safeguards - Countermeasures, controls put in place to avoid, detect, counteract, or minimize security risks to physical property, information, computer systems, or other assets. Safeguards help to reduce the risk of damage or loss by stopping, deterring, or slowing down an attack against an asset.

Sensitive data - Data that is encrypted or in plain text and contains PII or PHI data. See PII and PHI above.

6.0 Revision History

Version	Date of Revision	Author	Description of Changes
1.0	August 17, 2016	SANS Institute	Initial version

Fair Use Policy – Online Content

This is a brief on fair use policy as explained by Rich Stim [24].

What is Fair Use Policy

What Is Fair Use?
A fair use is any copying of copyrighted material done for a limited and "transformative" purpose, such as to comment upon, criticize, or parody a copyrighted work. Such uses can be done without permission from the copyright owner. Most fair use analysis falls into two categories: (1) commentary and criticism, or (2) parody.

Commentary and Criticism
If you are commenting upon or critiquing a copyrighted work — for instance, writing a book review — fair use principles allow you to reproduce some of the work to achieve your purposes. The underlying rationale of this rule is that the public reaps benefits from your review, which is enhanced by including some of the copyrighted material.

Parody
A parody is a work that ridicules another, usually well-known work, by imitating it in a comic way.

Practice Question 9

Reviewing the examples of IT/IS policies in this chapter,
outline the key components of a policy.

....

....

....

....

....

....

....

....

....

....

....

....

....

....

....

....

CHAPTER SUMMARY

The chapter explored a diversity of information systems policies from a diversity of institutions and organizations. These examples tend to demonstrate that the development and usage of policies are rather specific to the context and purpose for which they were developed. As such, policies are developed to respond different information systems needs and uses in an organizational context. While some policies are developed to govern general behavior, others tend to be more specific, governing network security, server security and application security. Further, there are policies or guidelines also developed for content management and usage on online platforms. Information systems managers therefore have daunting task of developing and keeping up policies to respond to organizational needs, technology trends and employee, customer and stakeholders' behavior.

Chapter 3 - IT/IS Policy Development and Implementation

The objective of this chapter is to enable readers/students understand the components of an IT/IS policy and apply an IT/IS policy development framework to develop an IT/IS policy.

COMPONENTS OF IT/IS POLICY

In this section, we will discuss and illustrate the components of IT/IS Policy. 12 components are discussed. However, their applicability in practice tend to differ. Not all policies, depending on the purpose and accessibility, tend to cover all the 12 components. Most companies tend to have key sections including the purpose, scope, authorization, the policy, and related standards/references. The order of components may also tend to differ across organizations.

Policy Information

The policy information details all the key information which describes the policy, standard or guideline. The information displayed are:

- Name of the Company, Firm or Organization, e.g: ABC Ventures
- Name of the Policy (broad category) e.g: Information Security
- Subject of the Policy (sub-category) e.g: Clean Desk Policy
- Policy Number (and perhaps version number) e.g: 3255 v2
- Effective Date (date the policy came into effect)
- Revised Date (date of revision)
- Status of Policy (approved, under consideration/review, draft et cetera depending on the status of the policy)

For example:

ABC Company Policy

INFORMATION SECURITY

NUMBER: 3255 v2
EFFECTIVE DATE: 11/05/2014

REVISED DATE: 11/08/2016

SUBJECT: CLEAN DESK POLICY

STATUS: APPROVED

Overview

What is the overall focus of this policy? The overview provides a summary of the policy, explaining the background to the policy and relevance. It may also provide information were the policy can be obtained.

For example: *Clean Desk Policy Overview*
The second objective of the information systems policy of ABC Company states that, the company shall responsibly collect, manage, protect and dispose of (where necessary) all sensitive and confidential information collated from its stakeholders, including employees, customers, senior management, vendors, government agencies and shareholders. In view of this, a clean desk policy seeks to ensure that all sensitive/confidential materials are removed from an end user workspace and locked away when the items are not in use or an employee leaves his/her workstation. It is one of the strategies which will be utilized to reduce the risk of security breaches in the workplace. Such a policy can also increase employee's awareness about protecting sensitive information.

Purpose/Rationale

What are the objectives of the policy? The purpose, rationale or objectives communicate the vision, strategy, and principles as they relate to the management and use of information and information technology resources, while supporting the core vision and goals of the company.

For example: *Clean Desk Policy Purpose/Rationale*
The purpose of this policy is to establish the minimum requirements for maintaining a "clean desk" – where sensitive/critical information about our employees, our intellectual property, our customers and our vendors are secure in locked areas and out of site. A Clean Desk policy is not only ISO 27001/17799 compliant, but it is also part of standard basic privacy controls.

Scope

What is the scope of the policy? Who and What does it apply to? Is it company-wide or affect a sub-unit or function of a company.

For example: *Clean Desk Policy Scope*
This policy applies to all ABC company employees and affiliates (Who). The policy applies to the keeping, management and processing of sensitive and confidential data/information, both in manual form and on computer (What).

Authorization

Whose is responsible for management (development, revision and interpretation of policy?

For example: *Clean Desk Policy Authorization*
The responsibility for IT policy management has been assigned to the Office of Corporate Information Systems (OCIS). This includes:
- Coordination of IT policy and underlying development, dissemination, and education;
- Review and analysis of existing policies for continued applicability and effectiveness; and
- Interpretation of current policy related to specific issues, situations and incidents.

Policy/Standards/Guidelines

The key statements which will spell out the policy, standards or guidelines are outlined in this section. It may be structured to accommodate the different issues, stakeholders and themes that need to be addressed.

For example: Clean Desk Policy Statements
A. Employees are required to ensure that all sensitive/confidential information in hardcopy or electronic form is secure in their work area at the end of the day and when they are expected to be gone for an extended period.
B. Computer workstations must be locked when workspace is unoccupied.
C. Computer workstations must be shut completely down at the end of the work day.
D. Any Restricted or Sensitive information must be removed from the desk and locked in a drawer when the desk is unoccupied and at the end of the work day.
E. File cabinets containing Restricted or Sensitive information must be kept closed and locked when not in use or when not attended.
F. Keys used for access to Restricted or Sensitive information must not be left at an unattended desk.
G. Laptops must be either locked with a locking cable or locked away in a drawer.
H. Passwords may not be left on sticky notes posted on or under a computer, nor may they be left written down in an accessible location.
I. Printouts containing Restricted or Sensitive information should be immediately removed from the printer.
J. Upon disposal Restricted and/or Sensitive documents should be shredded in the official shredder bins or placed in the lock confidential disposal bins.
K. Whiteboards containing Restricted and/or Sensitive information should be erased.
L. Lock away portable computing devices such as laptops and tablets.
M. Treat mass storage devices such as CDROM, DVD or USB drives as sensitive and secure them in a locked drawer.

N. All printers and fax machines should be cleared of papers as soon as they are printed; this helps ensure that sensitive documents are not left in printer trays for the wrong person to pick up.

Policy Compliance

Who shall ensure compliance to the policy? Who qualifies for exemptions? What are consequences of non-compliance? This section is relatively optional. It could be dropped from a policy document which is aimed at being shared publicly.

For example: Clean Desk Policy Compliance
Compliance Measurement

The Office of Corporate Information Systems (OCIS) team will verify compliance to this policy through various methods, including but not limited to, periodic walk-throughs, video monitoring, business tool reports, internal and external audits, and feedback to the policy owner.

Exceptions

Any exception to the policy must be approved by the OCIS team in advance.

Non-Compliance

An employee found to have violated this policy may be subject to disciplinary action, up to and including termination of employment.

Related Standards, Policies and Processes/References

If the policy is related to or references another organizational governing mechanism, such information should be outline in this section.

For example: Clean Desk Policy References
ABC Company Code Section 314

314.5 – Document Protection Policy

Definitions and Terms

Provide glossary in this section. In some cases, definition and terms is placed at the beginning of the document after the table of contents.

For example: Clean Desk Policy Definitions
Clean Desk refers to an uncluttered desk, void of sensitive/confidential document.

Service: Dissemination and Maintenance

Dissemination

Dissemination outlines the strategies to make the policies readily accessible to stakeholders.

Maintenance

Maintenance outlines the strategies to revise and maintain polices.

For example: Clean Desk Policy Service
Dissemination: This policy would made be readily accessible to all employees and other stakeholders defined in the scope. Multiple communication methods will be employed to widely disseminate policies, standards and guidelines, namely:

- Educational Seminars by OCIS
- Print – via OCIS, ABC Public Affairs, ABC Human Resources Department
- Electronic via ABC website

Maintenance: These guidelines as presently set forth, and as they may be amended from time to time, are binding on stakeholders defined in the scope. Revisions to the policies should be initiative by or through the OCIS.

Revision History

Outline all maintenance activities pertaining to the policy.

For example: Clean Desk Policy Revision History

Date of Change	Responsible	Summary of Change
June 2014	OCIS Policy Team	Updated and converted to new format.

POLICY DEVELOPMENT PROCESS

IT/IS policy development is usually a daunting task, especially as IT/IS become increasingly pervasive in organizations. It seems there is a need for policy, standard, or guideline for every activity in which IT/IS is applied or used. As a result, the process for developing IT/IS may also differ depending on the activity in which the IT/IS is being used and the firm/organization. In this section, we will evaluate generic steps which can guide the process and also provide some guiding principles to aid the IT/IS policy development process.

Steps for Developing and Revising/Updating IT/IS Policy:

1	Initiate and establish structures	▪ Decide on the triggers for policy development or review ▪ Decide on who will have responsibility for developing this policy ▪ Establish a co-ordinating group, if considered necessary.
2	Review and Research	▪ Study relevant resource documents and legislation in the firm, industry, nation and where necessary global ▪ Review existing practice or policy in firm. ▪ Identify the issues that need to be addressed.
3	Preparation of draft policy	▪ Templates can be adopted and modified with respect to the context of the firm
4	Circulation/ Consultation	▪ Circulate the draft policy and consult the relevant key stakeholders identified in the scope including the subject matter experts and non-subject matter experts ▪ Amend the draft policy, as necessary, in light of the consultation process.
5	Ratification and Communication	▪ Present the policy to the board of management for ratification. ▪ Make provision for the communication and circulation of the policy, or a statement of the key elements of the policy, to all stakeholders
6	Implementation	▪ Implement the provisions of the policy. ▪ Ensure that employees who handle, or have access to, information and information technologies (relevant to the policy) are fully familiar with the policy.
7	Monitoring	▪ Check that the policy is being implemented (e.g. by conducting periodic audits of procedures) and identify any issues arising.
8	Review, Evaluation and Revision	▪ Review and evaluate the impact of the policy at a pre-determined time, taking into account feedback from the stakeholders and other developments. ▪ Revise as necessary, in light of the review and evaluation process.

Adapted from [25]

IT/IS Policy Development Principles

Based on the eight step policy development process, we now ask the question, what principles underpin this process? The University of Michigan offers answers to this question. The university outlined the following guiding principles for development and maintenance of IT/IS policies, namely [26]:

Exhibit 9 The University of Michigan IT Policy Development Framework Principles

Initiation Criteria: Policy work shall be initiated when there is a compelling need for new or revised policy. Triggers may include new technologies, new laws or regulations, or operational or compliance needs that are not appropriately covered by existing policies or guidance.

Initiation Process: Policies and guidance shall be credible, implementable, enforceable, and sustainable. Impact analysis on both IT systems and end-users should be included in the policy planning and review processes.

Action-Oriented Living Document: Any unit may request consideration of new IT policies or changes to existing policies that apply university-wide; the process to be followed for such consideration is outlined in this IT policy development and administration framework.

Decentralization and Centralization Development Approach: IT policy development will be accomplished via individual workgroups convened to address specific topics. Each team will include appropriate subject matter experts. The unit responsible for the IT policy development and implementation will provide a central coordination function to ensure consistency and to address policy dependencies.

Interactive and Transparent Development: Process The policy development process will be transparent. Input from stakeholders will be addressed and/or incorporated throughout the process. Preliminary/interim policies and guidelines will be posted and disseminated to solicit feedback.

Flexibility with Focus on Functionality: The policy development process will be flexible. Circumstances may necessitate the publishing of best practices as a stop-gap to provide immediate guidance while a policy is being developed, vetted, and approved. In other cases, a policy may be established with detailed guidance to be provided at a later time.

Implementation and Interpretation: University-wide policies should be considered a floor, not a ceiling. Unit-level policies, guidelines, standards, or procedures may be developed to supplement university-wide guidance. They must meet the minimum criteria set forth in university-wide policies and related guidance, but may be more restrictive.

Practice Question 10

Compare and contrast the components of IT/IS policy outlined in this chapter with any IT/IS policy of an African institution of your choice.

....

....

....

....

....

....

....

....

....

....

....

....

....

....

....

....

CHAPTER SUMMARY

The chapter discussed 12 components of IT/IS policies and 8 steps to develop IT/IS policy. The twelve components are policy information, overview, purpose/rationale, scope, authorization, the policy/standards/guidelines, compliance, related standards/guidelines, definitions and terms, service (dissemination and maintenance) and revision history. In practice, some firms rephrase these components and not all the twelve may be represented in every policy in the firm. However, the key components which matter are generic. In order to develop IT/IS policies, eight steps are proposed as a guide. These steps may be implemented within seven principles, which spell out the critical factors (flexibility, transparency, decentralization, collaboration et cetera) which underpin a successful policy development process.

Chapter 4 - IT/IS Strategy

The objective of this chapter is to enable readers/students understand the IT/IS strategy and interrelationships with a business model. It will also enable readers/students to understand the components of IT strategy and apply that knowledge in the development of an IT/IS strategy.

DEFINING IT/IS STRATEGY

IT/IS Strategy defines how organization will use IT/IS to achieve its organizational objectives and goals. IT/IS strategy is therefore, ideally, IT/IS focused on the core goals of the organization, but its application is dependent on the organization's understanding of IT/IS and willingness and commitment to invest in IT/IS and use it to either support and/or drive its goals and objectives. According to Applegate [27]

> A business model defines how an organization interacts with its environment to define a unique **strategy**, attract the **resources** and build the capabilities required to execute the strategy, and create **value** for all stakeholders.
>
> **Strategy** is a **series of choices** that determine the opportunities you pursue and the **market potential** of those opportunities.

This said, we can deduce about strategy and IT/IS strategy:

1. Strategy is supposed to be a response to a business model (interaction of an organization with its environment in manner that create value). Hence, IT/IS strategy, a sub-set of organizational strategy, is supposed to serve a business model.
2. Strategy is nothing without the capability to achieve it. Strategy relies on capabilities, IT/IS strategies also relies or needs IT/IS capabilities to be functional.
3. Strategy should lead to value creation, IT/IS strategy should therefore contribute to that value creation process and possibly seek to sustain it.
4. Strategy involves choices which are opportunities that have a market potential. IT/IS strategy should support or drive the pursuit of a selected opportunity or set of opportunities.
5. Strategy is no value without a pursuit; IT/IS strategy can make or should be able make that pursuit 'easy'.

6. Since strategy involves choices, strategy should have some relative flexibility to quickly adapt to changes in an organization's interaction with its environment; IT/IS strategy should be flexible to adapt to changes in business priorities and resources/capabilities (financial/budgets, human resources/skills, customer needs et cetera).

So when an organization makes choice of a particular opportunity that has a market potential, we can say that a strategy has been developed or the firm has defined a particular orientation to commit resources and create value. **Strategic Orientation** reflects

> the firm's **perception** of the **profitable opportunities** that it can **'see' or strategically evaluate** in its business environment and is **willing** to take advantage of with respect to its existing and 'obtainable' resources [28]. This is the productive opportunity of the firm.

For strategy to be successful, firms should have the capability to perceive or 'see' or strategically evaluate correctly or further to consistently 'see' and avert any threats to the current strategy. Here again, IT/IS strategy can play role. For example, IT/IS applications can be used to capture and evaluate consumer preferences and real-time so as to inform strategic decision making (see Exhibit 10).

Exhibit 10 Amazon and Big Data

In health care, everyone talks about Big Data. But petabytes of data is only as good as your ability to operate on it. Amazon is a master at using big data. Amazon has a global network of more than 100 fulfillment centers, the positioning of which are informed by analyzing and optimizing with data. Every day, Amazon monitors its network and decides where to open centers. It also analyzes consumer preferences and creates algorithms that stock popular items at different areas of the warehouse, making staff members more efficient [29].

However, there is more. Amazon also uses Big Data to monitor, track and secure its 1.5 billion items in its retail store that are laying around it 200 fulfilment centres around the world. Amazon stores the product catalogue data in S3. This is a simple web service interface that can be used to store any amount of data, at any time, from anywhere on the web. It can write, read and delete objects up to 5 TB of data each. The catalogue stored in S3 receives more than 50 million updates a week and every 30 minutes all data received is crunched and reported back to the different warehouses and the website [29].

Role of IT/IS Strategy

IT strategy matters. It matters for several reasons. First, IT strategy enables a firm to define and establish it plans (mid-to long term) for planning IT/IS investments and introducing IT/IS into a business or organizations. These plans will describe the resources needed – information, human, processes, architecture, infrastructure and policies – and how they can be aligned to business objectives. Second, IT strategy can be become the source of competitive an advantage. This is possible if IT is used to strategically to drive or enable strategic activities in an organization. The use of IT/IS in organizations, particularly for commerce, can generate benefits categorized as; strategic, informational and operational [31] (see Exhibit 11). Hence, IT/IS strategy defines and established the way by which a firm can use information and information technology resources to obtain these benefits.

Exhibit 11 Potential Benefits of IT/IS in Business

1. Strategic
   a) Extending the firm's market reach.
   b) Product/Service differentiation.
   c) Loyalty and retention of trading partners.
   d) Improved revenue/Access to New revenue.
2. Informational/Relational
   e) Improved marketplace information - relevance, volume and speed of access.
   f) Improved communication and relationships - Reforming *structural processes* - the removal of intermediaries and deepening of transactional relationships.
   g) Improved internal access to information for tactical and strategic decisions.
   h) Enhanced *trading processes* - informed decision-making, uncertainties and asymmetries are removed
3. Operational
   i) Reduced transactional costs.
   j) Time efficiency.

Operational benefits are associated with the reduction in coordination costs in delivery of products, goods and services in the market place. Firms will be able to communicate directly with potential customers and trading partners on the availability of goods and services. Information on the quality, quantity and delivery times of goods can be exchanged. This may contribute to reduction in costs of searching for goods, services, buyers and sellers; reduction in delivery and inventory costs especially for perishable products; reduction of risk in frequent long journeys for goods; and increase in the timeliness in decision-making, negotiating and fulfilling transactional terms. Achieving operational benefits can build up to relational benefits.

Relational benefits are associated to the benefits of improved communication and relationships between actors involved in a transaction. For example, the ubiquity, localization and personalization features of new and emerging technologies (like mobile/location-based devices) can lead to disintermediation where firms may bypass or avoid, 'middlemen' and shorten distribution channels to transact directly with potential customers and trading partners. This improved and direct communication may increase the motivation and confidence and understanding between firms and their customers and trading partners. These relationship benefits may build up to strategic benefits.

Strategic benefits are associated with benefits which increase the market "reach" (access new markets) and the performance of firms. Operational and relational benefits can build up the trust for market participants – customers, suppliers and other trading partners - to engage in long term relationships in the good of all. These benefits include the deepening of relationships, loyalty and retention between firms and their customers and trading partners; product and service differentiation and personalization; and increase in the "reach" through improved reputation, recommendations and referrals. In effect, increase in market reach could stimulate the growth and performance for the firm.

Though all these three benefits tend to be interrelated (a firm can achieve one benefits while trying to achieve another), a firm can start from operational benefits and orient its strategies and streamline its processes to achieve informational and strategic benefits.

Strategic Use of IT/IS by Nike

Practice Question 11

Designing your own running shoes on a computer and having them arrive in a box a few weeks later is the sort of thing that is both futuristic and mundane, all at once. Nike iD was launched in way back in 1999. It was Futuristic, because the idea of Nike iD alone - the very conceit - that you can boot up a computer, design a pair of shoes in a few seconds and send them off to a big factory where someone, a robot ideally, will sew, package and send them to your door exactly as you requested. The customer becomes the designer as they change and add a personal look and feel to a selected item. The service can be accessed both online from their homepage and in physical branches (called NIKEiD Studios) which are situated in parts of Canada, France, England, Main Land Europe, China and the USA. In total, NIKEiD has 102 studios where customer can access the customization design service [32] [33].

Analyzing NIKEiD, what can you say about Nike's IT strategy and what benefits is the company deriving from it.

Reflection on IT/IS Strategy ....

....

....

....

....

....

....

....

....

....

NIKEiD IT/IS Benefits ....

....

....

....

....

....

....

....

....

....

....

....

....

....

....

....

....

....

....

STRATEGIC INFORMATION SYSTEMS PLANNING

What It Is and Why It Matters

The above example from NIKEiD tends to illustrate that the strategic use of IT/IS benefits can be sometimes an intentional process which involves planning how to use IT/IS to enable or drive the strategic objectives or priorities of a firm. This planning process is termed strategic information systems planning (SISP) or information systems strategic planning (ISSP). Plans connote a thought process to outline endeavor and perhaps assess the cost and resources needed to accomplish such an endeavor. Thus, plans are primarily, deliberate, requires discipline and commitment, involves the making of decisions and outlining of actions of what has to be done and why it is has to be done. SISP is therefore a deliberate, focused effort to define and establish fundamental decisions and actions that guide how IT/IS drive or support what an organization is, what it does and why does it [34]. A good SISP process will focus on the following areas [35] [36]:

• Business – Information Systems Alignment	*Which will require*	Information Systems Policy and Strategy
• Leveraging IT for Competitive Advantage	*Which will require*	Information Systems Policy and Strategy
• Efficient and Effective and Responsible Management of IS Resources	*Which will require*	Information Management Policy and Strategy
• Develop IT Architecture and IT Infrastructure	*Which will require*	Information Technology Policy and Strategy

By focusing on these areas SISP become relevant to an organization's quest to,
a) **Align IS with business needs:** SISP focuses on IT/IS strategy and this strategy has to be aligned with the business strategy in order support the achievement of business goals and objectives.
b) **Seek competitive advantage from IT:** Since SISP focuses on strategy (a series of choices), there is a specific strategy, that if well defined, can enable a firm gain a superior advantage in the marketplace. SISP therefore becomes a process which enable a firm to define its competitive IT strategy and implement it. For example, NIKEiD can be considered as a classic use of IT to create a competitive advantage.
c) **Gain top management commitment:** In many organizations top management tend to sign off all major projects – allocation of financial and human resources. Since IT/IS projects require investment of resources, it is important to demonstrate the business value of all key IT/IS projects. The answer to the business value lies in SISP. A good SISP will should assess the business value IT/IS resources to warrant investment.

d) **Forecast IS resource requirements:** A good SISP examines the immediate, mid and long term and evolutionary IT/IS needs of a firm. This information guides the firm in its budget allocation for IT/IS for a given financial year and also determines the priorities in IT/IS investments.

e) **Establish technology policies:** A good SISP goes beyond acquisition of IT/IS resources to establishes the measures to ensure efficient, effective and responsible usage of these resources.

© Pixabay

In precis, SISP enables firms to establish a clear vision for its immediate, mid and long term investment and usage of IT/IS resources consistent with its business strategy, goals and objectives. Such a process requires a critical examination of a firm's business environment – internal and external – to identify their strengths and weakness, as well as current and emerging external opportunities and threats.

The result is a roadmap [strategies, policies, guidelines, actions] of measurable strategies for attaining business goals, gaining competitive advantage and improving performance.

Approaches to SISP

Literature tends to discuss a number of different approaches to SISP [35] [36] [37]. Some of these practices are formal methods and best practices. Others are somewhat undefined or to say, informal. However, the common perspective across these approaches is the fact that, they can be evolutionary (dynamic and undergo change as they are implemented) [37] and the processes of planning are equally important to the process of implementing the plans [35]. An approach, as used here,

> may comprise a mix of procedures, techniques, user-IS interactions, special analyses, and random discoveries. There are likely to be some formal activities and some informal behavior ([35], p. 189).

To begin, Lederer and Sethi [37] identified four popular SISP approaches or methodologies to carry out SISP, namely Business Systems Planning; PROplanner; Information Engineering, and Method/1.

Business Systems Planning

Business Systems Planning (BSP), developed by IBM, involves top-down planning with bottom-up implementation. From the top-down, the SISP team first recognizes its firm's business mission, objectives and functions, and how these determine the business processes. It analyses the processes for their data needs. From the bottom-up, it then identifies the data currently required to perform the processes. The final BSP plan describes an overall information systems architecture comprised of databases and applications as well as the installation schedule of individual systems. BSP places heavy emphasis on top management commitment and involvement. [37]

PROplanner

PROplanner developed by Holland Systems Corp. in Ann Arbor, Michigan, helps planners analyze major functional areas within the organization. They then define a Business Function Model. They derive a Data Architecture from the Business Function Model by combining the organization's information requirements into generic data entities and broad databases. They then identify an Information Systems Architecture of specific new applications and an implementation schedule. PROplanner offers automated storage, manipulation, and presentation of the data collected during SISP. PROplanner software produces reports in various formats and levels of detail. A data dictionary (a computerized list of all data on the database) permits planners to share PRO planner data with an existing data dictionary or other automated design tools. [37]

Information Engineering

Information Engineering (IE), by Knowledge Ware in Atlanta, provides techniques for building Enterprise Models, Data Models, and Process Models. Managers participate in a critical success factors (CSF) inquiry, a technique for identifying issues that business executives view as the most vital for their organization's success. The resulting factors will then guide the strategic information planning endeavor by helping identify future management control systems. IE provides several software packages for facilitating the strategic information planning effort. However, IE differs from some other methodologies by providing automated tools to link its output to subsequent systems development efforts. For example, integrated with IE is an application generator to produce computer programs written in the COBOL programming language without hardcoding. [37]

Method/1.

Method/1, the methodology of Andersen Consulting (a division of Arthur Andersen & Co.), consists of ten phases of work segments that an organization completes to create its strategic plan. The first five formulate information strategy. The final five further formulate the information strategy but also develop action plans. A break between the first and final five provides a top management checkpoint and an opportunity to adjust and revise. Method/1 follows a layered approach. The top layer is the methodology itself. A middle layer of techniques supports the methodology and a bottom layer of tools supports the techniques. Examples of the many techniques are focus groups, Delphi studies, matrix analysis, dataflow diagramming and functional decomposition. Method/1, in precis, focuses heavily on the assessment of the current business organization, its objectives, and its competitive environment. It also stresses the tactics required for changing the organization when it implements the plan. [37]

These popular approaches tend to emphasize some key factors relevant for SISP success: internal and external business understanding (requirements analysis), need for software, and the need for consensus building through stakeholder consultations and interactions. There is also an emphasis on the dynamism in the implementation of plans to accommodate organizations changes introduced by the SISP, congruence between inputs to the planning (requirements analysis) and output (implementation strategies and actions), financial resources to acquire software/consultants who may understand these methods, and top management commitment.

These factors presuppose that several organizational factors tend to influence the SISP success and the manner in which the organization manage these factors (method issues, process issues and implementation issues) will determine the outcome of the SISP process.

Another set of approaches proposed by Earl [35] is summarized as follows:

Business-led

The analysis of business plans to identify how and where IT/IS can most effectively enable these plans to be implemented (often called a 'top-down' approach). The assumption is business planning should drive SISP. Business plans or strategies are analyzed to identify where information systems are most required. Information systems are seen as a strategic resource, and the IS function receives greater legitimacy. The challenge here is, business strategies are sometimes not detailed or are basically vague about details of the process. Hence, it is difficult for IS managers to specify IS needs - further analyses may be needed. Top management also delegate the details to SISP specialists, hence, they can be less ownership. The process involves the study of business documents, and interviewing of managers in order to develop proposals on IS implications on business plans. Since the emphasis is on top-level management input and business plans, views users and line manager are often less likely to be represented. IS strategy may be well aligned but less owned.

- o **Advice**: Good approach but ensure stakeholder involvement. Consultants may not always have best interests at heart. Ensure stakeholder buy-in (bottom-up) and top management understanding.

Method driven

The use of techniques – often a consultant's methodology – to identify IS needs by analyzing business processes and objectives. Often begins with an IS manager who believes that a method or technique will be best in convincing top management to consider IS needs and opportunities. This leads to the quest for the best method, which could be elusive. Consultants, engaged to introduce a method approach, may also lack business understanding or use a method which is a poor fit to the business structure and plan. Reliance on consultants means that they tend to have substantive influence on recommendations and thus, internal stakeholders/users may have less ownership to the SISP plan. Skeptical users and misconceptions may also polarize the firm and lead to poor acceptance of the SISP plan. The result is the SISP plan loses credibility and it is never fully implemented. On the other hand, some of the formal methods may show discrepancies in the business strategies and plans, which may help the firm if they are addressed before SISP process is completed.

- o **Advice**: Potentially good approach for some formal organizations, but ensure stakeholder involvement. Methods are not the panacea to poorly formulated business plans and strategies. Consultants may not always have best interests at heart. Ensure stakeholder buy-in (bottom-up) and top management understanding. The method have to be well explained to all key stakeholders and users.

Administrative

This entails the establishment of an IT capital and expense budget to satisfy approved projects (essentially a 'wish list' approach). The emphasis is on resource planning and allocation. IT/IS are viewed as a resource that has to be planned like other organizational resources. Formal procedures and wider managing planning and control procedures are therefore used to steer the SISP process. Business units submit IS development proposals to committees who examine them. This may be done alongside the firm's normal financial planning or capital budgeting routine. This is often a bottom up approach and hence IS is not viewed strategically but more operationally. On the other hand, the process may be viewed to be transparent and all users have opportunity to submit proposals. IT/IS resources are allocated in congruence with other activities and complementary resources can be allocated in parallel. That is, the SISP procedure has to be seen as part of company policy and procedures manual. SISP is therefore a friend of the internal administrative procedures.

- o **Advice**: Potentially good approach for some formal organizations where IS is viewed to be supportive and not strategic. Business unit should have the capacity of identifying strategic IS resources needed and make a business case. Steering committee may need to evaluate the strategic priorities of the firm alongside the evaluation of submissions from business units. Negotiation skills may also be needed by all parties – committee and business units.

Technology driven

The development of IT architectures as a foundation for expected application needs (equivalent to our interpretation of IT strategy, and sometimes called a 'bottom-up' approach). The emphasis is on developing an information systems-oriented model where a formal method is applied based on mapping the activities, processes, and data flows of the business. The focus is to derive architectures or blueprints for IT and IS, and often requires Information Engineering terminology. Architectures for data, computing, communications, and applications might be produced, and computer-aided software engineering (CASE) might be among the tools employed. This is often good when developing high level IT infrastructure in which blueprints have to be developed and adhered to closely. It is therefore demanding in terms of the resources, time and effort required. These demands often lead to frustration and impatience in waiting for a functional system.

- o **Advice**: Good approach for high level IT infrastructure. But ensure resources, time and effort are adequately available. The approach is beneficial if deliverables are well defined and somewhat decentralized or factored down to smaller applications.

Organizational

The identification of key themes for IT/IS projects – such as critical success factors for IT/IS projects. The emphasis is SISP is a continuous integration of the IS function and the organization. SISP can be unstructured and a 'not neat and tidy' endeavor. The plurality of methods in this approached is embraced - use the method that best fit a given purpose in the SISP process. The process of the SISP matters here - management understanding and involvement and allowing the organization to learn as it implements SISP. Hence, SISP may start from two themes or business objectives - improving customer service or product development. These themes are broken to identifiable and frequent deliverables. Then, teams are set to investigate and process how the objective will achieved. The presence of an IT executive in the team will allow for the understanding of why, where and how IT/IS can help. Thus team work is critical to the development of IT/IS strategy which will support the business objectives. IT/IS strategies often emerge from ongoing organizational activities, such as trial and error changes to business practices, and continuous and incremental enhancement of existing applications. This may lead to challenges as to how themes are determined, segmented IT/IS infrastructure which respond to themes and not necessarily to an organizational wide architecture. An organization may adopt Rockhart (1979)'s Critical Success Factor (CSF) technique in this approach. CSFs are key areas, usually less than 10 for an organization, where things must go right for the organization to flourish [38]. The technique is used for understanding more clearly the objectives, tactics, and operational activities in terms of key information needs of an organization and its managers, and strengths and weaknesses of the organization's existing systems [39].

- o **Advice**: Good approach to ensure organization learning through SISP. May be appropriate for firms which have an established IT/IS strategy and plan and may need to develop another IT/IS to respond to an emerging or new theme or business need. Hence, the new plan builds on existing IT/IS plans, strategies and infrastructure.

Exhibit 12 SISP Approaches Compared

	Business-Led	Method-Driven	Administrative	Technological	Organizational
Emphasis	Business	Technique	Resources	Model	Learning
Basis	Business plans	Best method	Procedure	Rigor	Partnership
Ends	Plan	Strategy	Portfolio	Architecture	Themes
Methods	Ours	Best	None	Engineering	Any way
Nature	Business	Top-down	Bottom-up	Blueprints	Interactive
Influencer	IS planner	Consultants	Committees	Method	Teams
Relation to business strategy	Fix points	Derive	Criteria	Objectives	Look at Business
Priority setting	The board	Method	Central committee	Compromise	Emerge
IS role	Driver	Initiator	Bureaucrat	Architect	Team member
Metaphor	It's common sense	It's good for you	Survival of the fittest	We nearly aborted it	Thinking IS all the time

[35]

STEPS OF INFORMATION SYSTEMS PLANNING PROCESS

Building on the approaches to SISP, we will now briefly evaluate outlines of different steps to carrying out SISP as proposed in literature and practice. The key question in our evaluation is how these steps relate to any of the approaches outlined in this chapter.

Common Steps in SISP

The SISP process consists of strategic awareness, situation analysis, strategy conception, strategy formulation, and strategy implementation [40]. These steps are also corroborated by other studies [39], hence the title common steps ins SISP.

Exhibit 13 IS Planning Phases and Tasks

Phase	Activities	Methods and Techniques
Strategic awareness Planning the IS planning process	Determine Key Planning Issues Define Planning Objectives Organize Planning Teams Obtain Top Management Commitment	Business System Planning (IBM)
Situation analysis – Analyze Current Environment	Analyzing current business systems Analyzing current organizational systems Analyzing current information systems Analyzing the current external business environment Analyzing the current external IT environment	Critical Success Factor Analysis (CSF) SWOT Analyses Porter's Competitive Forces Model PEST Model Porter's Value Chain Analyses
Strategy conception Conceiving strategy alternatives	Identifying major IT objectives Identifying opportunities for improvement Evaluating opportunities for improvement Identifying high level IT strategies	Business System Planning (IBM) Method/1 PROplanner
Strategy formulation Selecting strategy	Identifying new business processes Identifying new IT architectures Identifying specific new projects Identifying priorities for new projects	Information Engineering Business System Planning (IBM) Method/1
Strategy implementation Planning strategy implementation	Justifying IT costs Defining change management approach Defining action plan Evaluating action plan Defining follow-up and control procedure	Net Present Value Return on Investment Breakeven Analysis Business Case Approach Business System Planning (IBM)

Adapted from Source: [41]

Rainer *et al.*'s Steps in SISP

Exhibit 14 Rainer et al. Steps in SISP

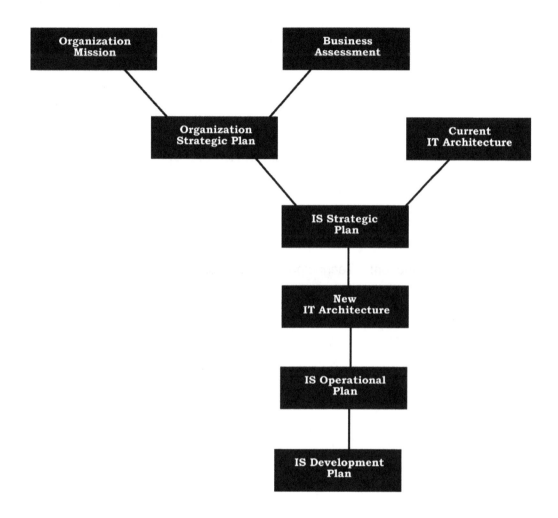

According to Rainer *et al.* [40], the IT/IS strategic plan begins with an assessment of an organization's strategic plan (mission and business assessment) and the its current IT architecture.

This assessment process informs the IT/IS strategic plan. IT/IS strategic plan is a set of long-range goals that describe the IT/IS infrastructure and identify the major IT/IS initiatives needed to achieve the organization's goals.

The **IT/IS strategic plan** must meet three objectives [41]:

a) aligned with the organization's strategic plan.

b) provide for an IT architecture that seamlessly networks users, applications, and databases

c) efficiently allocate IS development resources among competing projects so that the projects can be completed on time and within budget and still have the required functionality.

After a company has agreed on an IT strategic plan, it next develops the **IS operational plan** that consists of a clear set of projects that the IS department and the functional area managers will execute in support of the IT strategic plan.

a) **Mission**: mission of the IS function (derived from the IT strategy)

b) **IS environment:** summary of the information needs of the functional areas and of the organization as a whole

c) **Objectives of the IS function:** best current estimate of the goals of the IS function

d) **Constraints on the IS function:** Technological, financial, personnel, and other resource limitations on the IS function

e) **Application portfolio**: prioritized inventory of present applications and a detailed plan of projects to be developed or continued during the current year

f) **Resource allocation and project management:** listing of who is going to do what, how, and when.

Ward and Peppard's Strategic Planning Framework

Ward and Peppard [41] have proposed IT Strategy Formulation and Planning framework which consists of three building blocks—inputs, outputs, and essential activities (Exhibit 15).

Exhibit 15 IT/IS Strategic Framework

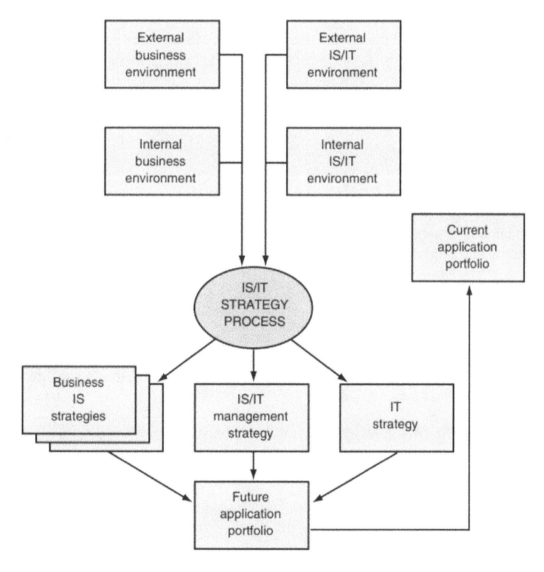

Source: [41]

The model consists of three building blocks—inputs, outputs, and essential activities. The inputs to Ward and Peppard's strategic planning framework are as follows:

- **The internal business environment:** current business strategy, objectives, resources, processes, and the culture and values of the business.

- **The external business environment:** the economic, industrial, and competitive climate in which the organization operates.

- **The internal IT environment:** the current IT perspective in the business, its maturity, business coverage, and contribution to attainment of the organization's goals (e.g., cost reduction), skills, resources, and the technological infrastructure. The current application portfolio of existing systems and systems under development, or budgeted but not yet under way, is also part of the internal IT environment.

- **The external IT environment:** technology trends and opportunities and the use made of IT by others, especially customers, competitors, and suppliers.

The outputs are:

- **IT management strategy:** the common elements of the strategy that apply throughout the organization, ensuring consistent policies where needed.

- **Business IS strategy:** how each unit or function will deploy IT in achieving its business objectives.

- **Application portfolios.** Alongside each of the business objectives are application portfolios to be developed for the business unit and business models, describing the information architectures of each unit. The portfolios may include how IT will be used at some future date to help the units achieve their objectives.

- **IT strategy:** policies and strategies for the management of technology and specialist resources.

The core attributes of the framework is focused on

- Flexible, modular, and able to pick up deliverables from earlier or parallel activities

- Emphasis on deliverables and Clear checkpoints

- Recognition of the interactive and cyclic nature of the process

- Recognition of the importance of the human side of the process

- Simple diagramming tools

Source: [41]

SISP Development Path

Despite the common steps in SISP, Galliers [44] argues that SISP may not happen overnight. It could be a process which entails various stages of growth (see Exhibit 16). This means organizations may evolve around a number of activities. However, Galliers does not provide any information on the actual processes undertaken during SISP activities.

Exhibit 16 SISP Development Path

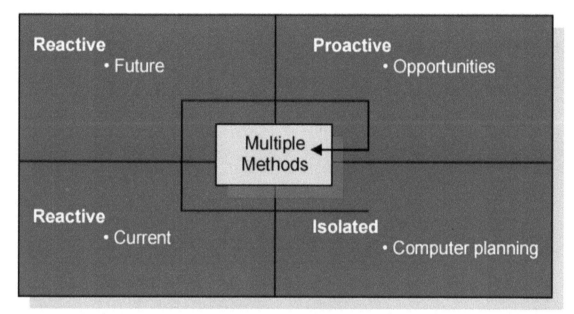

Source: [44]

Mcfarlan IT Strategic Grid

Nolan and McFarlan [45] proposed the Strategic Grid, which facilitates the evaluation of the relationship between IT strategy and business strategy and operations. This model analyzes the impacts of IT-existent applications (present) and of an applications portfolio (future), defining four boxes, each one representing one possible role for IT in the enterprise: "Support," "Factory," "Turnaround," and "Strategic." The strategic grid explains where and how IT investment has been made. It classifies IT investment into four categories [45] [46]:

Exhibit 17 Mcfarlan IT Strategic Grid

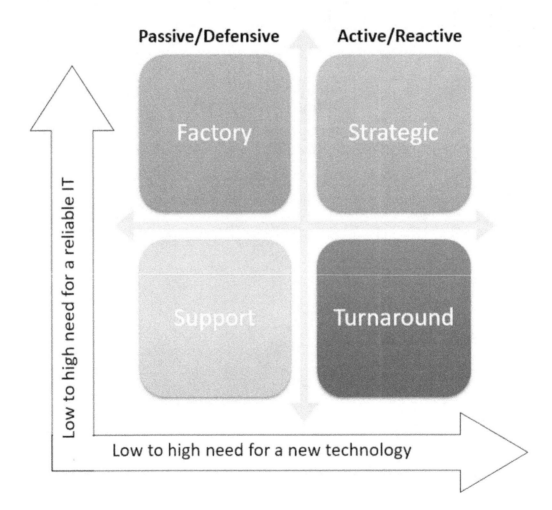

Strategic: Investment that is critical for future success.

- High operational impact, high strategic impact. IT/IS strategy is the backbone of competitive success. New IT/IS applications in development are crucial to future competitive success.
- IT/IS organizations that have most projects in this quadrant understand that IT/IS can both improve core operations of the firm while simultaneously generating strategic options. The IT/IS budget will be very significant
- E.g.: Bank, retail stores, airlines

Turnaround: Investment in IT/IS applications which may be important to achieving future success.

- Low operational impact, high strategic impact. This quadrant is about exploiting new technologies to provide strategic opportunities.
- IT/IS supports operations but are not dependent on IT/IS absolutely. New IT/IS applications necessary to enable the firm to achieve its strategic objectives
- The systems that have being planned and developed may be critical to the firm's survival or growth. However, there is uncertainty as the capabilities of the company in terms of delivery and support are untested
- IT/IS investment is increasing –perhaps rapidly
- E.g.: High Fashion, Oil refining

Factory: Investment in IT/IS applications which the organization currently depends for success.

- Low operational impact, high strategic impact. This quadrant is about exploiting new technologies to provide strategic opportunities.
- IT/IS is critical to current operations but is not at the heart of the company's strategic development. IT/IS is enabling critical operations to function smoothly
- Future IT/IS applications are not the critical factor for future business success
- The IT/IS budget will always be significant
- E.g: Defense, Government and immigration

Support: Investment in IT/IS applications which are valuable but not critical to success.

- Low operational impact, high strategic impact. This quadrant is about exploiting new technologies to provide strategic opportunities.
- IT/IS supports operations but are not dependent on IT/IS
- New IT/IS applications are not necessarily linking to business planning activity.
- IT/IS is used essentially for administrative systems to improve internal efficiency
- IT/IS investment is average / below average
- E.g: Universities and Consultants

The classification helps management to see whether IT/IS investments so far have been aligned to business objectives such as to support business growth, competitiveness or new business venture.

IT/IS SUCCESS

Building on the work of Venkatraman and Ramanujam [45], Segars and Grover [46] developed a four dimensional instrument to measure the success of SISP: alignment, analysis, cooperation and capabilities.

Alignment refers to the results of the linkage of the IS strategy and business strategy, analysis refers to the results of the study of the organization's processes, procedures, and technologies, and cooperation refers to the results of the general agreement about development priorities, implementation schedules, and managerial responsibilities. The fourth dimension, capabilities represented the improvement in the potential of the planning system. [40] [46]

Exhibit 18 SISP Success Measure

Alignment
Understanding the strategic priorities of top management
Aligning IS strategies with the strategic plan of the organization
Adapting the goals/objectives of IS to changing goals/objectives of the organization
Maintaining a mutual understanding with top management on the role of IS in supporting strategy
Identifying IT-related opportunities to support the strategic direction of the firm
Educating top management on the importance of IT
Adapting technology to strategic change
Assessing the strategic importance of emerging technologies

Analysis
Understanding the information needs of organizational subunits
Identifying opportunities for internal improvement in business processes through IT
Improved understanding of how the organization actually operates
Development of a 'blueprint' which structures organizational processes
Monitoring of internal business needs and the capability of IS to meet those needs
Maintaining an understanding of changing organizational processes and procedures
Generating new ideas to reengineer business processes through IT
Understanding the dispersion of data, applications, and other technologies throughout the firm

Cooperation
Avoiding the overlapping development of major systems
Achieving a general level of agreement regarding the risks/tradeoffs among system projects

Establishing a uniform basis for prioritizing projects
Maintaining open lines of communication with other departments
Coordinating the development efforts of various organizational subunits
Identifying and resolving potential sources of resistance to IS plans
Developing clear guidelines of managerial responsibility for plan implementation

Capabilities

Ability to identify key problem areas
Ability to identify new business opportunities
Ability to align IS strategy with organizational strategy
Ability to anticipate surprises and crises
Ability to understand the business and its information needs
Flexibility to adapt to unanticipated changes
Ability to gain cooperation among user groups for IS plans

Practice Question 12

Unilever Transforms Its Digital Marketing Services

Source: [49]

About Unilever

Unilever was formed in 1930 by the merger of Dutch margarine producer, Margarine Unie and British soap maker, Lever Brothers. Today, the consumer goods giant sells food, home care, refreshments, and personal care products in over 190 countries. Unilever has headquarters in London, United Kingdom and Rotterdam, the Netherlands, and subsidiaries in over 90 countries. The company employs more than 170,000 people. In 2012, Unilever reported more than €51 billion in revenue.

The Challenge

Unilever North America in Englewood Cliffs, New Jersey needed to re-design its infrastructure to support Unilever's digital marketing approach. Unilever previously used on-premises data centers to host its web properties, all of which had different technologies and processes. "We needed to standardize our environment to support a faster time-to-market," says Sreenivas Yalamanchili, Digital Marketing Services (DMS) Global Technical Manager. Unilever optimizes its business model by testing a marketing campaign in a pilot country. If the campaign is successful, the company deploys it to other countries and regions. The IT organization wanted to use the cloud to implement the same process.

Why Amazon Web Services

After a comprehensive RFP and review process involving more than 16 companies, Unilever chose Amazon Web Services (AWS). Unilever's priorities in choosing a digital marketing platform included flexibility, a global infrastructure, technology, as well as a rich ecosystem of members. "With AWS, we have the same hosting provider for all regions, which means we don't have to customize and tweak hosting solutions per region," says Yalamanchili. "Unilever is focused on delivering great brands to consumers; it's not an IT shop. We're able to spend less and get more innovation by working with AWS and members of the AWS Partner Network."

The Unilever IT team had two goals for the AWS migration: deliver a common technology platform for websites with regional content delivery architecture, and migrate existing web properties to the cloud.

To develop the platform, Unilever attended an AWS workshop to design the architecture. Then the DMS team built a pilot platform (a disaster recovery site for third-party hosting in Miami) for stakeholder review. After obtaining business approval, Unilever chose CSS Corporation, an Advanced Consulting Partner member of the Amazon Partner Network (APN), for system integration and application development. The DMS team worked with CSS to develop a global content management system (CMS) . The CMS platform lets agencies build brand web sites globally and publish them across several AWS regions. Unilever uses a HAProxy load balancer to improve performance of its web sites and runs its databases on Microsoft SQL Server and MySQL.

For disaster recovery, Unilever stores backup data, snapshots, product and recipe media files in Amazon Simple Storage Service (Amazon S3), and uses EBS Snapshot Copy to copy Amazon Elastic Block Store (Amazon EBS) snapshots from the US East (Northern Virginia) Region to the US West (Northern California) Region. "We designed a disaster recovery solution to protect our content management system, content deployment architecture, and many GOLD-classified web properties—and to give the business confidence in the AWS Cloud," says Yalamanchili. Analyzing NIKEiD, what can you say about Nike's IT strategy and what benefits is the company deriving from it.

Unilever and CSS created Amazon Machine Images (AMIs) running Windows and Linux for use on approximately 400 Amazon Elastic Compute Cloud (Amazon EC2) instances. Amazon Virtual Private Cloud (Amazon VPC) provides flexibility for deployments and access to the Internet. Nick Morgan, Enterprise Architect for Digital Marketing comments, "What's nice about using AWS is how easily we're able to scale the instances based on the nature of a campaign's popularity. We used Auto Scaling as well as manual scaling for sites such as Recipedia.com and Axeapollo.com. We can deploy instances across different AWS Regions and Availability Zones and use Amazon EBS snapshots to bring services back."

To migrate its web properties to the cloud, Unilever built pre-production and production environments on AWS for several existing websites. Once Unilever's creative and production agencies certified the website in the pre-production environment, Unilever switched the DNS address for production environment to go live on AWS.

After a successful pilot launch, Unilever migrated more than 500 web properties from its data centers to AWS in less than five months. Since then, Unilever has more than 1,700 web properties running on AWS worldwide. "Throughout our business globally, we strive to create repeatable models and it's easy to standardize our hosting environment with AWS," says Yalamanchili. "If a marketing campaign that we deploy in the US East (Northern Virginia) Region is successful, we can easily replicate it to Asia Pacific (Singapore) Region for the APAC countries."

CSS supplied Unilever with machine images of different operating systems, APIs and tools to automate the process of launching a new project. "The way CSS automated launching instances reduced the time to launch a project by about 75 percent," says Morgan. "What used to take four days now only takes one day. We're not rebuilding web and database servers from the ground up all the time. We can just clone and re-use images."

The Benefits

For Unilever, moving to the AWS Cloud improved business agility and operational efficiency. "Previously, requesting a website for a marketing campaign was a lengthy process," says Yalamanchili. "By using AWS, we improved time to launch for a digital marketing campaign from two weeks to an average of two days. That's more than seven times faster than our traditional environment. If a brand manager has an idea, he or she can implement it before the competition,"

"Using AWS saves us time," he continues. "I can simply go to the AWS website and plug in numbers to calculate costs. That makes it easy for me to set up a standard billing model for websites. It takes our partner, CSS, less than 12 hours to calculate pricing for a campaign website. I can comfortably say to my marketing folks that we have the capacity for anything we want to do. We can focus on innovation rather than infrastructure."

"The other advantage is the responsiveness of the AWS Cloud," says Yalamanchili. "By using AWS, one of the brand managers was able to completely alter a campaign within 24 hours, which wouldn't happen with the physical infrastructure."

"AWS listens to us and helps come up with ideas to do things differently that are beneficial," says Morgan. "I really enjoy the rapid rate of innovation from AWS." Yalamanchili adds, "With AWS, it's the customer's way, always. AWS has proved to us that it's the customer that matters by listening to us and innovating products and services."   source: [49]

Reflecting on the Unilever case study, answer the following questions:

1. Analyze the SISP approach using Earl's SISP approaches.

2. What are the critical factors which led to IT/IS success?

Reflection on SISP Approach ....

....

....

....

....

....

....

....

....

....

....

....

....

....

....

....

Reflection on Critical Success Factors of Unilever Case Study.................................

....

....

....

....

....

....

....

....

....

....

....

....

....

....

....

....

....

....

IT/IS-BUSINESS ALIGNMENT

What is IT/IS- Business Alignment? How is it achieved? Is it even achievable? How do you know whether a firm's IT/IS is well aligned with it?

Just as businesses are dynamic, any attempt to align IT/IS with Business will be a dynamic. Business-IT alignment or IT/IS business alignment refers to this dynamic state where business institute measures to effectively use IT/IS to support the achievement of its business objectives. Business-IT alignment or IT/IS business alignment is one of the core priorities of strategic information systems planning.

Now, that we understand Business-IT alignment or IT/IS business alignment, let us explore how it is achieved and even if it is ever achievable. There are several approaches, models and techniques postulated by both academics and practitioners on how IT/IS business alignment can be achieved. There also seems to be no consensus on the best one. Hence, in this book, we will examine two of the popular approaches/model which arguably tends to be the basis of other models. The models are known as the Strategic Alignment Model (SAM) of Henderson and Venkatraman [50] and the IT Business maturity assessment model of Luftman [51].

Strategic Alignment Model

Henderson and Venkatraman's model suggests that four strategic domains are critical to IT-business alignment and linkages have to be built among them [50]. Strategic Alignment can only occur, when three of the four strategic domains are in alignment:

- Business Strategy; IT Strategy; Organizational and infrastructural processes; and Information Technology infrastructure and processes.

Organizations have to continuously seek alignment amongst these four domains, with particular attention to the strategic integration/fit (connection of the strategy and infrastructure, for both business and IT) and functional integration (connection of business and IT strategy and the business and IT infrastructure). The SAM model is illustrated schematically in Exhibit 19.

Exhibit 19 Strategic Alignment Model

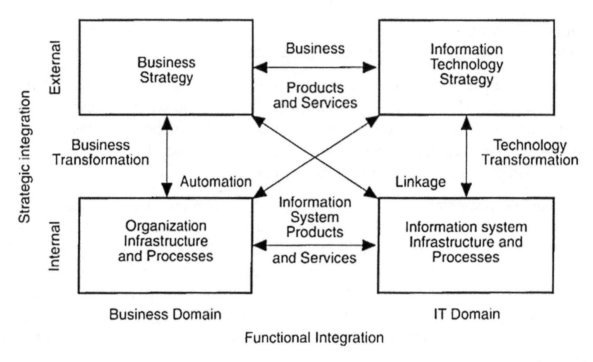

Source: [52]

The SAM model aids organizations in identifying the components of alignment or what needs to be aligned but quite silent on how that alignment will be achieved. That gap tends to be addressed by Luftman's IT Business maturity assessment model [50].

IT Business Alignment Criteria and Model

Luftman developed an IT business Alignment Criteria and Model in order to explain the following:

   a. How can organizations assess alignment?

   b. How can organizations improve alignment?

   c. How can organizations achieve mature alignment?

The author argues that alignment has involves determining the appropriate and timely way, of using IT/IS in harmony with business strategies, goals and needs. Luftman developed strategic alignment model which outlines 12 elements of Business/IT-Alignment [51]. The 12 elements focus on the activities that management need to perform to achieve cohesive goals across information technology and other functional organizations (e.g., accounting/finance, and marketing). The elements of this model are in concert with the prior research on enablers/inhibitors of IT-business alignment [53].

Exhibit 20 Components/Elements of IT-Business Alignment

I. BUSINESS STRATEGY

1. **Business Scope** – Includes the markets, products, services, groups of customers/clients, and locations where an enterprise competes as well as the competitors and potential competitors that affect the business environment.

2. **Distinctive Competencies** – The critical success factors and core competencies that provide a firm with a potential competitive edge. This includes brand, research, manufacturing and product development, cost and pricing structure, and sales and distribution channels.

3. **Business Governance** – How companies set the relationship between management, stockholders, and the board of directors. Also included are how the company is affected by government regulations, and how the firm manages its relationships and alliances with strategic partners.

II. ORGANIZATION INFRASTRUCTURE & PROCESSES

4. **Administrative Structure** – The way the firm organizes its businesses. Examples include central, decentral, matrix, horizontal, vertical, geographic, federal, and functional.

5. **Processes** - How the firm's business activities (the work performed by employees) operate or flow. Major issues include value added activities and process improvement.

6. **Skills** – H/R considerations such as how to hire/fire, motivate, train/educate, and culture.

III. IT STRATEGY

7. **Technology Scope** - The important information applications and technologies.

8. **Systemic Competencies** - Those capabilities (e.g., access to information that is important to the creation/achievement of a company's strategies) that distinguishes the IT services.

9. **IT Governance** - How the authority for resources, risk, conflict resolution, and responsibility for IT is shared among business partners, IT management, and service providers. Project selection and prioritization issues are included here.

IV. IT INFRASTRUCTURE AND PROCESSES

10. **Architecture** -The technology priorities, policies, and choices that allow applications, software, networks, hardware, and data management to be integrated into a cohesive platform.

11. **Processes** - Those practices and activities carried out to develop and maintain applications and manage IT infrastructure.

12. **Skills** – IT human resource considerations such as how to hire/fire, motivate, train/educate, and culture.

Source: [51]

The twelve components of IT-business alignment form the building blocks for the Luftman's strategic alignment maturity assessment method [50]. The model consists of 6 alignment areas, each of which has multiple attributes. For each area there are clearly defined maturity levels. All areas need to be given attention to mature the alignment between business and IT.

The six IT-business alignment criteria are illustrated in Exhibit 21: Communications Maturity, Competency/Value Measurement Maturity, Governance Maturity, Partnership Maturity, Scope & Architecture Maturity, and Skills Maturity.

Exhibit 21 IT-Business Alignment Criteria

COMMUNICATIONS

- Understanding of Business by IT
- Understanding of IT by Business
- Inter/Intra-Organizational
- Learning
- Protocol Rigidity
- Knowledge Sharing
- Liaison(s) effectiveness

COMPETENCY/VALUE MEASUREMENTS

- IT Metrics
- Business Metrics
- Balanced Metrics
- Service Level Agreements
- Benchmarking
- Formal Assessments/Reviews
- Continuous Improvement

GOVERNANCE

- Business Strategic Planning
- IT Strategic Planning
- Reporting/Organization Structure
- Budgetary Control
- IT Investment Management
- Steering Committee(s)
- Prioritization Process

SIX IT BUSINESS ALIGNMENT MATURITY CRITERIA

PARTNERSHIP

- Business Perception of IT Value
- Role of IT in Strategic Business Planning
- Shared Goals, Risk, Rewards/Penalties
- IT Program Management
- Relationship/Trust Style
- Business Sponsor/Champion

SCOPE & ARCHITECTURE

- Traditional, Enabler/Driver, External
- Standards Articulation Architectural Integration:
  - Functional Organization
  - Enterprise
  - Inter-enterprise
- Architectural Transparency
- Flexibility Managing Emerging Technology

SKILLS

- Innovation, Entrepreneurship
- Locus of Power
- Management Style
- Change Readiness
- Career crossover
- Education, Cross-Training
- Social, Political, Trusting Environment

Source: [50]

The above criteria is used alongside a five-levels or phases of strategic alignment maturity:

- Initial/Ad Hoc Process; Committed Process

- Established Focused Process; Improved/Managed Process

- Optimized Process

Each of the five levels of alignment maturity focuses on the set of six criteria. But before we explore the different levels, let us establish an understanding of each of the six criteria.

A number of questions have been shared by Coster [54] to guide how to examine the six criteria.

Communications: How well does the technical and business staff understand each other? Do they connect easily and frequently? Does the company communicate effectively with consultants, vendors and partners? Does it disseminate organizational learning internally?

Competency/Value Measurement: How well does the company measure its own performance and the value of its projects? After projects are completed, do they evaluate what went right and what went wrong? Do they improve the internal processes so that the next project will be better?

Governance: Do the projects that are undertaken flow from an understanding of the business strategy? Do they support that strategy?

Partnership: To what extend have business and IT departments forged true partnerships based on mutual trust and sharing risks and rewards?

Scope & Architecture: To what extend has technology evolved to become more than just business support? How has it helped the business to grow, compete and profit?

Skills: Does the staff have the skills needed to be effective? How well does the technical staff understand business drivers and speak the language of the business? How well does the business staff understand relevant technology concepts?

Luftman [51] notes that the procedure for assessing maturity is as follows:

1. Each of the criteria is assessed individually by a team of IT and business unit executives to determine the firm's level of strategic maturity on this criterion. In other words, each of the six criteria is found to be at either level 1, level two, level three, level four, or level five.

2. The evaluation team converges on a single assessment level for each of the six criteria. The discussions that ensue are extremely valuable in understanding both the current state of the organizations alignment maturity and how the organization can best proceed to improve the maturity.

3. The evaluation team, after assessing each of the six criteria from level one to five, uses the results to converge on an overall assessment level of the maturity for the firm. They apply the next higher level of maturity as a roadmap to identify what they should do next.

Based on the assessment, an organization may be found in one of these levels summarized in Exhibit 22:

Exhibit 22 Strategic Alignment Maturity Summary

Level 1 Initial/Ad-Hoc Process

COMMUNICATIONS: Business/IT lack understanding

COMPETENCY/VALUE: Some technical measurements

GOVERNANCE: No formal process, cost center, reactive priorities

PARTNERSHIP: Conflict; IT a cost of doing business

SCOPE & ARCHITECTURE: Traditional (e.g., accounting, email)

SKILLS: IT takes risk, little reward; Technical training

Level 2 Committed Process

COMMUNICATIONS: Limited business/IT understanding

COMPETENCY/VALUE: Functional cost efficiency

GOVERNANCE: Tactical at Functional level, occasional responsive

PARTNERSHIP: IT emerging as an asset; Process enabler

SCOPE & ARCHITECTURE: Transaction (e.g. Executive Support Systems)

SKILLS: Differs across functional organizations

Level 3 Established Focused Process

COMMUNICATIONS: Good understanding; Emerging relaxed

COMPETENCY/VALUE: Some cost effectiveness; Dashboard established

GOVERNANCE: Relevant process across the organization

PARTNERSHIP: IT seen as an asset; Process driver

SCOPE & ARCHITECTURE: Integrated across the organization

SKILLS: Emerging value service provider

Level 4 Improved/Managed Process

COMMUNICATIONS: Bonding, unified

COMPETENCY/VALUE: Cost effective; Some partner value; Dashboard managed

GOVERNANCE: Managed across the organization

PARTNERSHIP: IT enables/drives business strategy

SCOPE & ARCHITECTURE: Integrated with partners

SKILLS: Shared risk & rewards

Level 5 Optimized Process

COMMUNICATIONS: Informal, pervasive

COMPETENCY/VALUE: Extended to external partners

GOVERNANCE: Integrated across the org & partners

PARTNERSHIP: IT-business co-adaptive

SCOPE & ARCHITECTURE: Evolve with partners

SKILLS: Education/careers/rewards across the organization

Source: [51]

Luftman [51] argues that alignment is dynamic and evolutionary, every organization will exhibit a unique experience. IT/IS and business have to adapt their strategies harmoniously. Achieving maturity in alignment requires strong top management support, good working relationship throughout the organization especially with business and IT/IS staff and strong leadership and ownership. Beyond maturity, there is also the challenge of sustaining alignment. Sustaining alignment requires maximizing alignment enablers and minimizing inhibitors (see Exhibit 23).

Exhibit 23 Enablers and Inhibitors of Strategic Alignment

Enablers	Inhibitors
Senior executive support for IT	IT/business lack close relationships
IT involved in strategy development	IT does not prioritize well
IT understands the business	IT fails to meet commitments
Business - IT partnership	IT does not understand business
Well-prioritized IT projects	Senior executives do not support IT
IT demonstrates leadership	IT management lacks leadership

source: [53]

WHEN IT IMPLEMENTATION GOES WRONG

BBC: The £100m Worth Digital Media Initiative Debacle

Contributed by Bernard Okyere and Stephen Boateng

"The BBC's Digital Media Initiative was a complete failure. License fee payers paid nearly £100 million for this supposedly essential system but got virtually nothing in return. The main output from the DMI is an archive catalogue and ordering system that is slower and more cumbersome than the 40-year-old system it was designed to replace. It has only 163 regular users and a running cost of £3 million a year, compared to £780,000 a year for the old system."

Hon Margaret Hodge MP, Chair of the British PAC

British Broadcasting Company

BBC is the world's oldest national broadcasting organization, established by royal charter in 1922. Headquartered at Broadcasting House in London, BBC employs over 23,950 staff in total, comprising mainly public sector broadcasting staff with others serving as part-time and contract staff. BBC is a publicly financed broadcasting company and the dominant force in TV and radio in the UK. It operates eight television channels offering a mix of programming that includes general entertainment, news, current affairs, and sports. The BBC also keeps the world informed through its BBC World Service radio network launched with broadcasts in 28 languages and provides comprehensive TV, radio, and online services.

Digital Media Initiative (DMI): An Overview

The Digital Media Initiative was a transformation program that involved developing new technology for BBC staff to create, share and manage video and audio content and program from their desktops. In February 2008, the BBC entered an agreement with Siemens, its strategic technology partner, for the provision of delivery of the DMI program. However, the contract was terminated by mutual agreement with effect from July 2009 and the BBC brought the DMI in-house in September 2009. A report in April 2011 by the BBC gave assurance of completion of the project within 2011 with no further delays. However, the BBC then failed to complete the DMI Program and in May 2013 cancelled it at a cost to license fee payers of £100 million.

DMI was a complex business transformation program aimed at transforming the way in which the BBC makes content for its audiences. This initiative required a strategic investment in infrastructure, people and production processes that supported both the BBC's creative vision and its technology strategy to standardize the production, storage and use of digital content across TV, radio and online.

The proposed system had three key elements:

Production Tools: This new software would enable production teams in some of the BBC's main television production divisions to share content for factual and current affairs television programs, carry out basic video editing at their desktops and save partially completed work. Production tools would also allow users to transfer rough edits between their desktops and the BBC's professional editing facilities, while retaining any detailed information (known as 'metadata') associated with the files.

Digital Archive: The digital archive would provide a new online digital store for finished television programs and other selected program-making materials and information. The BBC's intention was to provide a more efficient alternative to storing archive material on magnetic tapes or other physical media. Production teams would be able to add detailed information (or 'metadata') about the content of digital files to make it easier to find archived material. The digital archive would be integrated with production tools to enable the automatic transfer of files and associated information between them.

Archive Database: The archive database would replace an existing system for cataloguing and managing physical archived content. The new system would be integrated with the digital archive to enable all BBC staff and third-party producers to search and order completed television program and related material held in the BBC's digital and physical archives.

The Challenge: Why the DMI Failed?

Poor Vision, Planning and Decision Making

Per the report of the National Audition Office (2014), as at 2012 there was no clear blueprint demonstrating the then required end state of the project. This could be taken as an indication of unclear objectives and limited knowledge on the rudiments of the project. The change over from Siemens, the multiple delays and false promises of completion goes to buttress the lack of a strategic plan and proper objectives and planning for the project. Interestingly, the BBC never sought for alternative and hence, it can be argued that the management tends to make hasty decisions. Reports on the issue reveal a dual lack of business and IT engagement contributing to the failure of the project. Indeed, the lack of competitive procurement for DMI, is also a sign of weak project and corporate governance.

Poor Risk Assessment and Management

Maylor (2010) asserted that risk is crucial because without being able to do so, those risks cannot be managed. To comprehend the risk level of a project depends on the knowledge on the project, Team expertise and inclusion of stakeholders (Maylor, 2010). However, it is noted that BBC has weak comprehension (of being confused) on the project, do not know about the approach employed by Siemens in dealing with the project, and even lacked clarity about the scope of technology releases (NAO, 2014). Very critical is the realization that BBC never learnt about why the project failed with Siemens in the very first stage.

The Issue of Complacency

The question many after the project cancellation was why the project managers thought they could complete the DMI in-house when Siemens could not. Evidently, this complacent attitude to the project contributed to its failure. According to Honorable Margaret Hodge,

"The BBC was far too complacent about the high risks involved in taking it in-house. No single individual had overall responsibility or accountability for delivering the DMI and achieving the benefits, or took ownership of problems when they arose."

Poor Oversight, Accountability and Reporting

The DMI did not provide clear and transparent reporting on progress against plan, cost to complete, or delivery of benefits to enable effective decision-making within the governance structure. Also, reporting on a quarterly basis to stakeholders meant that the reported status of DMI lagged behind the current status at the point the reports were considered. The report by the National Audit Office indicated that;

"The governance arrangements for the DMI were inadequate for its scale, complexity and risk. The BBC did not appoint a senior responsible owner to act as a single point of accountability and align all elements of the DMI. Reporting arrangements were not fit for purpose".

In effect, there was no independent view on the risks DMI faced in delivery of the solution and realization of the benefits. The BBC cancelled the DMI without examining the technical feasibility or cost of completing it, said the NAO.

Practice Question 13

In terms of strategic IS planning, what do you think led to the failure of DMI?

....

....

....

....

....

....

....

....

....

....

....

....

....

....

....

....

....

....

....

....

....

....

....

....

....

....

....

....

....

....

....

....

CHAPTER SUMMARY

The chapter discussed the role of IT/IS strategy and how IT/IS strategy is planned and aligned to business strategy. We learnt that SISP enables firms to plan how to use IT/IS in a manner that facilitates competitive advantage, gain top management commitment to IT/IS investment, forecast requirements and establish technology policies. The different approaches to SISP was explored and the steps of the planning process as discussed by a number of authors were also explained. We established that IT/IS business alignment is one of the core priorities of strategic information systems planning. Alignment is dynamic and evolutionary, every organization will exhibit a unique experience. IT/IS and business have to adapt their strategies harmoniously and achieving maturity in alignment will require strong top management support, good working relationship throughout the organization especially with business and IT/IS staff and strong leadership and ownership. Moreover, maximizing alignment enablers and minimizing inhibitors will ensure the sustainability of alignment.

To conclude, we need to understand that, so far as business are dynamic entities operating in a relatively dynamic and volatile business environment, and IT/IS is also evolutionary, perfect alignment is state that is often elusive. But being agile and responsive – possessing dynamic capabilities – will enable managers to steer their firms to a state of *near* perfect alignment.

Chapter 5 - Examples of IT/IS Strategies

The objective of this chapter is to enable readers/students understand the components of IT/IS strategy. The chapter also showcases examples of IT/IS strategies to enable readers/students to understand how the components are applied in practice.

GARTNER'S IT STRATEGY TEMPLATE

Gartner, Inc. (NYSE: IT) is one of the world's leading information technology research and advisory company that delivers technology-related insight and research to organizations. According to Gartner [55], IT strategy is about

> … how IT will help the enterprise win. This breaks down into IT guiding the business strategy, and IT delivering on the business strategy.

An IT strategy template is recommended to consist of

- A one- to two-page **board summary**, a 15- to 20-page **strategy document**, an **IT strategic plan** and an **IT operating plan**.

Exhibit 24 Gartner's IT strategy Template

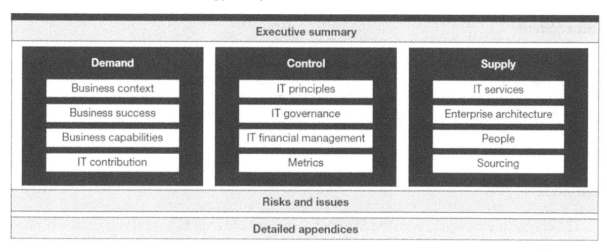

The IT strategy should contain sections on demand, control and supply (Exhibit 24).

Demand refers to the business context, how the business will win, what business capabilities are needed and how IT will contribute to that success.

Control outlines the mechanisms for making the strategy come to life, including principles, governance, financial management and metrics.

Supply details which services will and won't be provided, how the enterprise architecture will migrate to support the required business capabilities, the development of human capital to meet business needs, and the strategic approach to sourcing.

Source: [55]

Gartner advises that the details of projects and programs should be captured in the strategic plan; and details of financial, technical and human assets should be captured in the operating plan.

STANFORD'S IT SERVICES STRATEGIC PLAN

Below is an extract from the 2012 Stanford University's IT Services Strategic Plan [56].

Stanford's mission is "seeking solutions to global problems and equipping our students with the education they need to become leaders in a complex and interrelated world."

IT Services supports Stanford's mission by delivering information technology to support research, learning, teaching, and advanced patient care. IT Services seeks to be a trusted advisor to the Stanford community, providing strategies and services that meet real business needs.

Future State

Access to your stuff from anywhere, backed by the technology and support you need.
We partner across Stanford to ensure that you, as a member of the Stanford community, always have the technology and capacity you need to get your work done, independent of location or platform. Our goal is to provide solutions that enable flexibility, with IT support that is available 24x7x365.

Rationale

IT Services must engage with the Stanford community to anticipate and support the IT needs of a multi-campus, world-class research university and medical institution.

Our support models need to be proactive and continuously available around the clock because Stanford is mobile and global. As a member of the Stanford community, you expect untethered, on-demand, and seamless access to the applications, services, and support you need to get your work done.

Our goal is ensure that the services we provide can meet campus needs for research computing, emerging pedagogy, advancements in patient care, and inter-department, inter-school, and inter-institutional collaboration. We must provide rapid, secure, and efficient delivery of the best innovations available in the market, and support those innovations through a variety of methods and channels.

Client Services

What you will be able to expect from IT Services
- Access anywhere from any device at any time, with a tailored experience based on your Stanford identity
- Access 24x7x365 to services, solutions, and support
- Secure access to the applications and data you need from your Stanford-managed device
- Secure, integrated access to the best technology, in the cloud and/or at Stanford
- Consistent data protection and security, in the cloud and/or at Stanford
- Rapid delivery of solutions that meet the broadest campus need while providing the best value
- All applications and services work on your mobile devices
- Integrated support for the communication and collaboration needs of Stanford's academic and medical communities
- Seamless transition between local computing resources and elastic cloud-based resources
- Shareable computing resources to meet growing research computing demand, across campus and the global research community
- Additional channels for end-user support available whenever you need that support
- Expanded business continuity and disaster recovery

Current Roadmap

Our near-term strategic imperatives

Access
- Continue improving the Stanford University wireless network by increasing capacity, performance, security, coverage, and ease of use
- Provide pervasive, seamless use of unified communications tools: integrated voicemail, email, text messaging, fax, chat, phones, and video-conferencing
- Improve indoor cellular coverage
- Extend a consistent Stanford identity and authorization experience to the network and to

the cloud

Mobility
- Make mobile devices "first class citizens" in Stanford's computing infrastructure, ensuring that they are secure, with the right software and the right applications
- Add functionality and security to all Stanford-managed devices

Infrastructure
- Continue migration to cloud-based collaboration tools, integrating new tools for use by the Stanford community
- Continue to consolidate and virtualize computing equipment to realize energy savings and reduce operating expenses
- Implement cloud-based computing and storage cycles
- Combine data center and cloud solutions for business continuity to ensure that critical business and communication activities can continue in the face of the significant on-campus disruption

Support
- Increase help options by expanding self-help tools, participating in community-driven special interest groups, and providing interactive, online support options
- Initiate a computational research program for Stanford
- Facilitate solutions that support changing pedagogical models, such as IP video conferencing for Stanford High School
- Simplify the experience of ordering, provisioning, and procuring services

Future Roadmap

Our longer-term strategic directions

Access and Mobility
- Offer multiple tiers of authenticated access based on your Stanford identity and managed device
- Broaden mobile device coverage and increase integration of Stanford/vendor cellular networks

Infrastructure
- Ensure that cloud services provide an experience that is tailored to you while protecting your privacy and personal data
- Ensure that all University computing needs can be met through off-campus solutions, minimizing or eliminating any IT disruption in the event of an on campus disaster
- Provide an ability to replicate and share research data
- Establish elastic and geo-diverse storage and computing models
- Deliver highly energy-efficient physical, virtual and cloud-based alternatives for campus clients in order to reduce or eliminate their need for local server rooms
- Provide a specialized research computing datacenter facility that supports extremely high-

density computing and data storage capacity, and directly supports investigators' future modeling and data analysis requirements

- Continue to integrate medical support systems and unified communications systems to improve the efficiency and collaboration of Stanford Medicine physicians, faculty, nurses, and staff

Support

- Provide 24x7x365 continuous support by consolidating all IT Support Desks
- Merge collaboration technology, interface design, support channels, and knowledge bases within IT interactions to create user experiences that enable the academic mission of the University
- Identify and provide the appropriate suite of services to support emerging on-line pedagogical models, as recommended by the Presidential Advisory Committee on Technology in Higher Education.

Source: [56]

Practice Question 14

1. Identify the components of the IT Services Strategy of Stanford University and discuss the relevance of each of the component.

2. Compare and contrast the assurances offered to different stakeholders by the strategy in the current and future roadmap.

Reflection on the Components of the IT Services Strategy ....

....

....

....

....

....

....

....

....

....

....

....

....

....

....

....

....

....

....

....

....

....

....

....

....

Assurances offered by the IT Services Strategy to different stakeholders   ……………

....

....

....

....

....

....

....

....

....

....

....

....

....

....

....

....

....

....

....

UNC STRATEGIC PLAN TEMPLATE

Below is an extract from the 2010-2015 University of North Carolina at Charlotte Strategic Plan Template for Information Technology Services [57].

I. Executive Summary

A. Mission and Goals

The mission of the department is to provide highly reliable Information Technology infrastructure, tools, and services to enable the University to achieve its Academic, Research and Administrative objectives. Our goals are:
1. Reliable and Secure Systems
2. Teaching and Learning Excellence
3. Technical Innovation
4. Staff Expertise and Professionalism
5. Cost-Effective Use of Resources
6. External and Internal Partnerships

B. Summary of Process for developing Goals

The process commenced with a review of the overall University and Academic Affairs objectives. The ITS Senior Leadership then mapped the goals and objectives of our internal departments with to align with those goals. We produced a concept map depicting common goals and themes from an internal perspective. The Senior Staff then conducted an external scan, looking at the IT Strategic Plans at other Universities for best practices and innovative ideas. Once the College Plans were published the ITS Senior staff analyzed their plans to determine internal ITS objectives and the methodologies to support them. We gathered feedback from our key IT peers across the University and clustered these needs into groups. We combined information we had gathered externally with our internally generated concept map. This clustering produced the overall Goals and objectives for the department. Action plans to achieve these goals were determined during an off-site retreat.

C. Summary of Major Goals

1. **Reliable and Secure Systems.** ITS will ensure that the technology infrastructure of the university is reliable, dependable and secure.
2. **Teaching and Learning Excellence.** The department will provide the tools and expertise to create an environment that supports high quality educational programs.
3. **Technical Innovation.** ITS will actively encourage the investigation of new technologies to support the mission of the University in a time of rapid and unremitting technological change.
4. **Staff Expertise and Professionalism.** The ITS department will create a diverse, service oriented culture that values individual development and teamwork.
5. **Cost-Effective Use of Resources.** ITS will provide the right technology at the right price in a manner aligned with stated University priorities.
6. **External and Internal Partnerships.** The Information Technology Services Department will be a trusted partner for technology use on campus and will support the service mission

of the University through active engagement in our region and state.

D. Summary of New Resources required to achieve New Goals

1. Funding for Network Replacement Project is essential for the completion of goals 1, 2, 3 and 4.
2. By the end of the planning period, the University will need to have solid plans for an on-campus 10,000 square foot data center in order to achieve goals 1, 2 and 4.
3. Maintenance and Operations funding for new buildings as they come online to support goal 1.
4. Funding of the Kennedy Renovation Project at $5.1M is necessary to ensure goals 3, 4, 5 and 6.

Source: [57]

II. Environmental Scan/ Updates Since Last Five –Year Strategic Plan

A. Assessment of cumulative progress in meeting goals in current strategic plan

Goal # 1: Facilitate direct access to electronic information and services anytime, anywhere.
Met. During this planning period we completed the implementation of Banner, a University Portal (49er Express) and an online reporting data warehouse (Report Central).

Goal # 2: Provide efficient, effective and quality IT Services for faculty, students, and staff.
Partially Met. We implemented campus-wide life cycle management for PCs, improved our ability to monitor our systems and implemented industry standard best practices for managing our work. Inadequate facilities and the lack of a standard replacement process for servers and network prevented us from achieving the level of efficiency and reliability necessary.

Goal # 3: Support the enhancement of teaching effectiveness and studentcentered learning in on-campus and on-line learning environments.
Met. The Center for Teaching and Learning through its emphasis on the Scholarship of Teaching and Learning has focused on effective teaching practices. They have deployed the appropriate electronic tools (Course Management Systems) to facilitate those objectives.

Goal # 4: Provide IT resources and services to support the University's Research agenda
Met. The University Research Cluster provides High Performance Computing to researchers across the campus exceeding 1.5million CPU hours per year.

Goal # 5: Deploy technology tools to improve the University's administrative processes
Met. Completed the Implementation of all contracted Banner modules and the deployment of the Data Warehouse (Report Central) and the 49'er Express Portal. Accomplished two major upgrades to the Banner system. Implemented a research administration post award

management system (SAM) and completed first set of web-based workflow projects (EGA).
Goal # 6: Provide a cost-effective, scalable IT Infrastructure.
<u>Partially Met.</u> The deployment of a new remote data center and the implementation of our virtualization strategy were not completed during the planning period. The campus network in its current configuration does not meet our objectives for scalability, reliability or cost effectiveness.

Goal # 7: Ensure a secure e-learning, e-Research, and e-Business environment.
<u>Met.</u> The University had no major IT security breaches during the planning period. We successfully completed all audits.

B. Environmental Scan/Updates of Challenges, Opportunities, and Obstacles

The IT environment for Higher Education today is vastly different from the environment of the previous period strategic plan assessment. The rate of technological change has increased at a seemingly increasing rate. Major trends that affect the ITS Strategic Plan include:

- Rise of consumer oriented technology (Gmail, Iphone, Skype, RateMyProfessor, etc)
- Changing communication patterns (email, chat, texting, social media, video)
- Emergence of Social Media as a dominant web application.
- Software as a Service replacing institutionally owned infrastructure.
- Virtualization replacing one-computer-one-application model.
- Dominance of mobile computing (of all sizes and shape) over desktop computing

There have also been changes in North Carolina that present both opportunities and Challenges since the last planning period.

- Budget reductions and constraints.
- Standardization efforts at General Administration related to common authentication
- plus the beginning of a standard Shared Service Banner implementation.

Finally, the University itself has evolved significantly since the last planning period.

- Increased emphasis on the importance of electronic tools to support teaching - including the appreciation for asynchronous tools.
- The emphasis on interdisciplinary projects.
- Increased numbers of students on a relatively stable employment base drives the need for creative thinking about how we use technology to improve our processes.
- The completion of the Charlotte Research Institute has increased the need for technical support staff in the networking group.
- The use of computational resources in research programs continues to expand.
  - Source: [57]

III. New Strategic Goals, Action Plans and Performance Outcomes

A roadmap to achieve each goal is proposed in the strategic plan. Goal One is used as an illustration in this book.

A. Department Goal #1: Reliable and Secure Systems.

B. Relationship of goal to next higher reporting unit goal: 1, 2, 5, 6, 8

C. Action plans to achieve goal:
A. Fully implement High Availability technologies for systems reliability and redundancy.
B. Create Reliable disaster recovery and business continuity capabilities.
C. Develop technology lifecycle replacement funding mechanisms for critical enterprise systems.
D. Implement a Network Modernization Plan to improve reliability and enhance service delivery.
E. Provide a more secure campus IT infrastructure.
F. Implement best practice standards for systems management to improve reliability and reduce unplanned outages.
G. Build an on-campus data center appropriate for a growing research university.

D. Effectiveness measures/methods to assess outcomes/goal attainment:
A. The number of unplanned outages decrease annually.
B. Disaster recovery and business continuity plans are documented and tested.
C. Critical production enterprise systems are within their expected service life.
D. The network provides satisfactory wireless coverage for students and improved reliability for faculty and staff.
E. No unauthorized data releases from centrally managed systems.
F. Changes to high risk systems are managed through the ITS change control process.
G. Planning and analysis are conducted to prepare for implementation of a new datacenter.

E. Assessment schedule to assess goal:
- Annual assessment of planned and unplanned downtime.
- Annual Security Assessment report.
- Annual user satisfaction survey.
- Network replacement project is completed by 12/31/2011
- Modern, on-campus Data Center space is available by 6/30/2015

F. Person/group responsible:
- Vice Chancellor: 1.c; 1.g
- Chief Technology Officer: 1.a, 1.d; 1.e
- Director of Enterprise Information Systems: 1.a;
- Director of IT Plans and Policies: 1.b, 1.f

G. Performance outcomes for goal:
Campus IT systems aggressively support the administrative, academic and research missions

of the university.

H. Resources Required:
- 1.d: Network replacement $12.5MM
- 1.g; $3MM

Annual Reporting Requirements
I. Annual progress assessment of performance outcomes

J. Follow-up plan to make changes as a result of assessment findings

Source: [57]

Practice Question 15

1. Identify the components of the IT Services Strategy of University of North Carolina and discuss the relevance of each of the component.

2. What is the impact of the environmental scan on Goal 1 of the IT Services Strategy of University of North Carolina?

Reflection on the Components of the IT Services Strategy   ....

....

....

....

....

....

....

....

....

Impact of the Environmental Scan on Goal 1 ....

....

....

....

....

....

....

....

....

....

....

....

....

....

....

....

....

....

....

....

GENERIC STRATEGIC INFORMATION TECHNOLOGY PLAN

The strategic information technology plan is a guide to how the organization will use information technology to help accomplish its goals. The plan may be created with a scope of up to 3 years and should be updated frequently. The plan is shared by Baylor University as a guide for strategic technology planning for non-profits [58].

Overview of Information Technology Plan

I. Includes facts about the organization (Organization history, no. of employees, annual budget)
II. Major changes you are planning for the organization
III. Timeframe covered by this technology plan
IV. Major business areas you are trying to improve with technology
V. Overall budget set aside for IT

Introduction

Organization Mission
Write the overall mission of the organization, what it seeks to do with its efforts.

Organization Description
Write a short paragraph in which you describe critical information about the organization.
I. Name I II. Founding year I III. Industry
IV. Specialization I V. Number of clients I VI. Number of full time employees
VII. Number of volunteers I VIII. Number of locations
IX. Geographical region served

Information Technology Planning Team
Record information about each person who contributed to the content of the document. Outline their position/title and their role on the team.

Organization Analysis

Current Business Processes
Describe each major business process in the organization that contributes to achieving your goal. Process descriptions can be in the form of a narrative, flow chart, table, etc.

Process Improvements
Describe improvements that can be made with the supporting use of technology. For example:
I. Which processes you would like to improve
II. Why you would like to improve them
III. How improvements can be made

Current State of Technology

Write down the present state of the organization's technology. This should be in either paragraph form or a bulleted list of sentences.
Indicate if:
I. There is a shortage or surplus of certain technology
II. Current technology does not fit the service you wish to provide
III. Specific systems are in need of updating, etc...

An inventory of all Technology (hardware/software) should be kept separate from the Strategic Technology Plan.

Technology Improvements and Acquisitions

Describe the technology improvements that are needed to support the business process improvements that were identified earlier. Be specific in listing the desired solution, the benefit it would produce and an estimate of the cost. It is important to get as much input from staff as possible when planning for your organization's technology needs.

Technology Budget

Write the overall annual budget amount the organization should dedicate to Technology. This amount should be consistent with your detailed IT Budget worksheet. The detailed IT Budget worksheet should be kept separate from the Strategic Technology Plan.

Measures of Technology Plan Success

Describe quantitatively and qualitatively how you will measure the success of your technology-supported process improvements.

Source: [58]

Practice Question 16

Using the above strategic IT plan, develop an IT strategy for a small and medium enterprise in your community. Your strategy should include an environmental scan of the business context of the enterprise.

Name of Enterprise

....

....

Organization Mission

....

....

....

....

....

....

Organization Description

....

....

....

....

....

....

....

....

....

....

Information Technology Planning Team

....

....

....

....

....

....

Organization Analysis

Current Business Processes

....

....

....

....

....

....

....

....

....

....

Process Improvements

....

....

....

....

....

....

....

....

....

....

Current State of Technology

....

....

....

....

....

....

....

....

....

....

....

....

....

....

....

Technology Improvements and Acquisitions

....

....

....

....

....

....

....

....

....

....

....

....

....

....

....

....

....

....

....

....

....

....

Technology Budget

....

....

....

....

....

....

....

....

....

....

....

....

....

....

Measures of Technology Plan Success

....

....

....

....

....

....

....

....

....

....

....

CHAPTER SUMMARY

The chapter explored examples of IT strategy for a number of different organizations. Through these examples, an understanding of the components of an IT strategy was established. Gartner's IT strategic template explained that IT strategy outlines how IT can help enterprises win. It advises that the strategy template should consist of one- to two-page board summary, a 15- to 20-page strategy document, an IT strategic plan and an IT operating plan. Primarily, the strategy document should focus on the strategic priorities and goals whiles details concerning the budget and how it is going to be achieved can be captured in the operating plan and strategic plan. The examples provided through Stanford University, University of North Carolina at Charlotte and Baylor University demonstrate that IT strategic plan goes beyond immediate strategic goals to define future strategic goals. The immediate goals therefore before the incremental steps which will lead to the future goals.

Chapter 6 - Linking Policy to Strategy: E-governance in Senegal

The objective of this chapter is to enable readers/students to explore the link between policies (e-governance) to strategic programmes to implement the policies. This is done through a case study on e-governance in Senegal. It is based on a research study carried out in 2011-2012 by the author of this book.

The themes covered are e-governance objectives and goals, e-governance policies, e-governance programmes and projects/initiatives, online presence of government institutions, impact of e-governance and gaps to be addressed.

E-GOVERNANCE OBJECTIVES AND GOALS

Electronic governance (e-governance) is about the use of ICTs as an enabler to continuously transform the internal and external relationships of governments, the public sector and other governance stakeholders and build citizen-centric, cooperative and polycentric modern governance.

Although there seem not to be clear-cut e-governance objectives in Senegal, the vision of "e-Senegal" driven by the Agency of State Information Technology (ADIE) has taken shape with the Programme for Modernization of Information Systems Administration (PMSIA) initiated by the government at the beginning of the year 2000. The Programme for Modernization of Information Systems Administration (PMSIA) seeks to promote the modernisation of major administrative functions of the state through information systems. The objective of e-Senegal, which is driven by PMSIA, is to increase access to government services and information by citizens – moving government to e-government and the citizen to an e-citizen. Nevertheless, the success of these objectives hinge on the provision of citizens with a minimum of tools tailored to their specific needs including points of access to ICT. This, therefore, requires the implementation of consistent and coordinated policies and programs as part of a coherent policy response towards the achievement of the set goals and objectives.

E-GOVERNANCE POLICIES

In support of the objectives of e-governance, the Senegalese government and other stakeholder organisations have developed policy initiatives to enhance the implementation and realization of the e-governance agenda. Exhibit 25 outlines the e-governance policy initiatives in Senegal. These policy initiatives include the National Program for Good Governance (PNBG), the Program for Modernization of Information Systems Administration (PMSIA), Vision E-Senegal and others which seek to promote e-governance and e-democracy in the country. Despite the fact that a number of policy initiatives have been formulated, most of them are still at the implementation stage and are yet to be passed.

For instance, even though the National Program for Good Governance (PNBG) was launched in 1999 under the original name of "Integrated Program for Public Sector Reform", to consolidate the democratization process and to strengthen rule of law and national capacity for development management, the status of this policy initiative is still 'in progress' and has not yet been completed. Other policy initiatives still in progress include vision e-Senegal and the Program for Modernization of Information Systems Administration (PMSI) which was initiated in early 2000 by the government.

Achievements of the Policies

The vision of e-Senegal, driven by the Agency of State Information Technology (ADIE) which seeks to increase e-government and e-citizen, forms the center stage upon which numerous policy initiatives have been instigated. Although, experts' opinion suggests that the various programs and projects related to the achievement of e-governance in Senegal have many deficiencies inherent in their accomplishments, the general feeling is that Senegal could do better given the potential at her disposal. For instance, the Coordinator of the ICT cluster and the Teleservices Accelerated Growth Strategy (SCA) opined that

> "the existence of large projects in teleprocedure, telehealth, e-education and so on...are all based on the use of ICT in governance. However, these projects have not yet reached interesting levels and, therefore, the implementation of e-governance at the national level cannot be said to be effective yet. Senegal, therefore, can do better, given the potential at its disposal, the infrastructure in place and potential in terms of available human resources".

Exhibit 25 E-governance Policies in Senegal (as of 2011)

Name of Policy	Brief Description	Implementing Agency	Status of the Policy As of 2011
1. Law No. 2001-15 of December 27, 2001 amended Code of Telecommunications	The amended code provides the telecommunications sector with an effective and transparent regulatory framework to promote fair competition in provision of services. The code also established telecommunications and Posts regulation agency (ARTP) in 2001.	Regulatory Agency for Telecommunications and Posts (ARTP)	Established
2. Programme National De Bonne Gouvernance (PNBG) 2003	This policy seeks to consolidate the democratization process and to strengthen the rule of law and national capacity for development management. It is also to promote economic growth based on transparent procedures for governance and the creation of an enabling environment for private sector development.	Government and National Institutions	In progress
3. Programme De Modernisation Des Systemes D'Information De L'Administration (PMSIA) 2000	The primary goal of this policy is to promote the modernisation of major administrative functions of the state through information systems.	Agency of State Information Technology (ADIE)	In progress
4. Vision "E-Senegal" (2002)	This policy initiative seeks to place the citizen and businesses in a centre stage of attention of government. The policy seeks to also allow all citizens access to information and to meet the performance needs of the state. Initially announced in a presidential speech in January 2002, but gained its implementation agency, ADIE, in July 2004.	Agency of State Information Technology (ADIE)	In progress
5. Decree No. 2004-1038 Agency of State Information Technology (ADIE)	This agency was created in 2004 by Decree No. 2004-1038 of 23 July 2004 with the mission to implement the strategy of e-government and e-Senegal.		Established
6. Other e-governance related Laws and policies established by ADIE	a. Law No. 2008-10 of January 25, 2008 on orientation law on information society b. Law No. 2008-08 of January 25, 2008 on electronic transactions c. Law No. 2008-11 of January 25, 2008 on Cybercrime d. Law No. 2008-12 of January 25, 2008 on the protection of personal data e. Law No. 2008-41 of August 20, 2008 on cryptology.	Agency of State Information Technology (ADIE),	Passed

In addition, the former Advisor to the Ministry of ICT shares the view that Senegal, as a nation, has made great efforts over the past ten years regarding e-governance including institutional and infrastructural developments. He further argues that

> "Senegal has set up an agency of the State Information (ADIE), which helps governments to access the Internet more simply and also to develop applications internally or to implement policy initiatives to facilitate ICT and everything related to digital services in the administration and services of interest to people. However, when Senegal is compared with countries like Morocco, Kenya, Rwanda and even South Africa, you realize that it really has a lot to do in relation to its objectives. When compared to the achievements, it appears that Senegal is seriously lagging behind".

As already stated above, although national policy initiatives have given rise to interesting practices in relation to e-governance, it is difficult to talk about a "success story" in the Senegalese context. This is because whereas most programs and projects were launched with great enthusiasm, they were quickly abandoned or were weakened by partisan political manoeuvring contrary to the ideals of the general public interest. However, some success has been chalked in the implementation of digital identity cards, the government intranet and the website for administrative procedures.

In line with this assertion, an ICT Consultant arouses that "in terms of e-governance in Senegal, there is not much to say, because it is now almost non-existent." This he justified by pointing out that

> "there are no applications and steps forward of the actions that were embarked on to reach more areas of e-government to make government more efficient, effective, internal and also in its relations with citizens. However, e-governance could have been steered in a direction that setup facilities to enable citizens to have their say on issues concerned with the administration and elected officials."

Challenges to the Effective Implementation of Policies

The effective implementation of the policy initiatives have been twisted and turned by some impediments. Prominent amongst these impediments include the lack of political strategy, insufficient infrastructure, and Human Resource challenge.

Lack of political strategy; A major challenge confronting the development of the telecommunications sector in Senegal and, in particular, e-governance applications, is the lack of political strategy. This is apparent by the remarkable discrepancy between the political speeches and achievements made in the field. For instance, the Coordinator of the ICT cluster and the Teleservices Accelerated Growth Strategy (SCA) proffers that

> "in the case of e-governance, a significant problem is the political factor that tends to neutralise any effort in the public interest. He further states that although a relevant initiative to address the deficiencies of public services was in progress, the project was suddenly abandoned as soon as the Director of the Regulatory Agency for Telecommunications and Posts (ARTP) was dismissed due to charges of financial malfeasance."

Another dimension of the lack of political strategy has to do with the duplication of effort on one side, and on the other side, projects housed at the Presidency or in government departments. In the words of a renowned ICT Consultant

> "there are many ICT policy initiatives and programme in the Senegalese context which are not widely dispersed. These policies and programs are also handled by a single agency (ADIE) which takes care of everything in the area of administration, state and connectivity. In conclusion, all these create duplication and inefficient initiatives in e-governance."

Finally, an ICT Consultant opined that

> "politicians generally appear disjointed and out of step with the advanced national realities. While they remain marked by illiteracy and poverty that prevent access and ownership of digital tools, no program is implemented to support the development of e-governance applications, hence the challenge."

Infrastructure; The needed infrastructure to support e-governance activities is inadequate and not fully deployed for the benefit of the general public. For instance, the digitization of some procedures in Senegal has not changed much in practice as a result of the lack of the needed infrastructure to cater for the changes. An ICT Consultant clearly articulates that

> "turning to biometric without knowing the next step of development is completely illogical and fruitless given the lists of electors. He further postulates that the costs associated are very high for such systems since the needed infrastructure to cater for them is not yet available."

Again, the issue of infrastructure poses a challenge to e-governance applications and services since fraudulent and malicious practices are not so far removed from the management of public affairs.

Human Resource Challenge; Effective implementation of policy initiatives to a large extent depends on how skilled the available human resources are and in the case of e-governance, the story is no different. It is, therefore, essential to develop national expertise in ICT especially among those policy makers who are responsible for the implementation of e-governance projects in Senegal.

For instance, because the success of such policies, programs and projects need the collective involvement of researchers and experts in the field to improve decision making, it becomes necessary to get the requisite human resources for the task at hand. According to an ICT Consultant,

> "the issue of human resources does not really arise because Senegal is full of talent able to think of ICT from a technical perspective. However, the challenge has to do with how to get and/or train human resources capable of thinking both technically and strategically to leverage technologies for e-government initiatives".

E-governance Programmes and Projects

Exhibit 26 outlines a selected number of key e-governance programmes and projects. The initiatives by government and other organizations aimed at enhancing the relationship between government and citizens include the National Programme for Good Governance (PNBG), Modernization Program Information Systems Administration (PMSI), Government Intranet Project, "Your paperwork", and SenGouv. The main objective of these e-governance projects is to increase or improve access to information. Arguably, none of the initiatives studied exceeds the first phase of the development of e-governance ("Phase 1") – which essentially aims to provide citizens information without the real possibility of interaction with public services. For example, the Agency of State Information Technology (ADIE) manages an online initiative known as "Your paperwork" (www.demarches.gov.sn). An ICT consultant noted that "this site is relevant in that it provides access to online forms; the building permit feature is already functional". The objective is to provide information in manner in which it is complete, timely and presented seamlessly to facilitate the implementation of administrative services. The Ministry of Interior also manages an elections monitoring website - www.elections.sn - that provides citizens with information on the elections, especially on the election register, electoral boundaries, the electoral code and the voting arrangements.

Concerning achievements, the programme PMSIA were cited by almost all interviewed experts to be a successful programme. The objective of the programme is to promote the modernisation of administrative functions of the state through information systems.

Exhibit 26 E-governance Programmes and Projects in Senegal

Name of Programme/Project	Brief Description	Implementing Agency	Status of the Project
1. Programme SAFI (Systeme Administration Des Formalites Informatisees)	Project Interchange System Administration Procedures (SAFI) is designed to meet two major goals. The first goal is to develop a model for managing remote procedures within the Senegalese administration. The second goal is to create a platform that can support the model developed. The first system, the filing of VAT Returns online, has been deployed since 2009. The second pilot system Safi is the request for authorization to construct, with the goal, reducing the time of delivery of deed within 28 days for simple cases and 40 days for complex cases.	Agency of State Information Technology (ADIE)	In progress
2. Project "Points E-Gov"	This policy was developed to identify points of access to government services by all citizens. The policy seeks to provide a focal point from which the citizens will be able to accomplish all of their current administrative procedures, whether a deposit or access of administrative records such as birth certificate, criminal record and national identity card. Finally, the policy is to provide solutions to the unequal distribution of government services and the low level of ownership and use of ICT in society.	Agency of State Information Technology (ADIE), ARTP	In progress
3. Project Intranet Gouvernemental (PING)	The PING project is to supply a broadband network for voice, video and data in order to decentralize access to information and quality services. The objective of the project is to extend the government intranet to other administrative services located in the interior regions of the country through the establishment of a broadband network in all parts of the country and to improve a conducive investment environment in Senegal.	Agency of State Information Technology (ADIE)	In progress
4. Vos demarches administratives www.demarches.gov.sn	The main objective of the "Your paperwork" website is to provide information in a manner which is complete, timely and presented seamlessly to facilitate the provision of administrative services. This is a state reform which intends to work for transparency and efficiency and the	Agency of State Information Technology (ADIE)	In progress

Name of Programme/Project	Brief Description	Implementing Agency	Status of the Project
	development of the internet in a way that is easier for the entire population to adopt.		
5. Journal official du Senegal www.jo.gouv.sn	This project has brought about improvement in the legal environment which has enabled the implementation of remote procedures on VAT by making available full texts of codes, agreements, laws, decrees and other official regulations to the general public. This has brought about efficiency and effectiveness in the provision of e-governance activities to the general public in a more cost effective way.	Agency of State Information Technology (ADIE)	Completed
6. Site web des elections aux Senegal www.elections.sn	This website for elections aims to predominantly facilitate procedures related to the organisation of parliamentary and presidential elections. The objective of this initiative is to provide citizens with information on the elections, especially on the election register, electoral boundaries, the electoral code and the voting arrangements.	Ministere de l'interieur	Completed
7. ORBUS: Systeme de collecte electronique des documents du commerce exterieur www.senegalpaperlesstrade.com	ORBUS, a technological infrastructure and a system of advanced services, is used to facilitate electronic communication between the various stakeholders in foreign trade.	Direction generale de la Douane et le GIE GAINDE2000	Completed
8. Consultation des resultants du Bac par SMS	The project facilitates real-time access to student results across the country by allowing parents to check and verify the results of their children. The system gives users the opportunity to send SMS and receive SMS as a reply without delays.	Office du Baccalaureat du Senegal	Completed
9. Delivrance de permis de peche et dímmatricuation des pirogues du Senegal www.manobi.sn	The project ensures better monitoring of the fisheries sector as well as the identification and registration of fishing boats. This project is a software solution used in the electronic tagging of canoes. It works by using a chip that provides the functions of registration card, fishing license on the map, mobility, PDA and other solutions for reading and controlling the electronic documents.	Direction des peches maritimes (DPM) et Societe Manobi Senegal	Completed
10. Marches publics au Senegal	This project is designed as a platform to ensure public participation within the	Agence de Regulation des	Completed

Name of Programme/Project	Brief Description	Implementing Agency	Status of the Project
www.marchespubl ics.sn	procurement process between suppliers, economic actors, and government departments, local authorities, national companies, companies. Its main objectives are to make public procurement transparent, to fight against bribery and corruption, and to promote healthy competition in a favourable business climate in order to attract both local and foreign investors.	Marches Publics (ARMP) et Direction Central des Marches Publics (DCMP)	
11. Services d'appui aux petites et moyennes enterprises www.senegal-entreprises.net	The aim of this portal is to support the development of SMEs in Senegal. The project seeks to provide vital information on strategies, business environment in Senegal as well as support institutions in tax payment, business registration and procedures for import and export.	Agence de Developpeme nt et d'Encadremen t des Petites et Moyennes Entreprises (ADEMPE)	Completed

An example is the launch of an administrative and government intranet in 2005. The intranet provides direct links to appropriate services while providing relevant information on work schedules, contact details and personal information of government employees. The information provided by the site is of interest to both individuals and associations, communities and businesses, merchants and students, professionals and the general public. The site does not target only residents and nationals, but also takes into account the concerns of the Senegalese in the diaspora and foreigners. They can access information about the immigration procedures including medical precautions before travelling to Senegal, differences between a residence permit and an authorization of transit, and procedures to obtain an ID card abroad.

Despite all these features, there is still some room for improvement. An ICT for Development consultant argued that "we are not in an era where you just make a website and put it online". This comment suggests some extra work that should be done possibly in educating the population in the use the website. There was a phenomenal increase in internet penetration in Senegal in 2011, internet subscribers increased by 130% total up to 15.7 per 100 inhabitants by December 2011 (ARTP, 2012). Such increase in internet penetration opens up opportunities to roll-out more interactive internet-ready applications, especially with mobile applications, as mobile internet users also increased by 680%. The use of low-cost technologies like mobile phones has the potential of extending services to reach resource-poor contexts in the country. A GIS expert explained that the challenge facing government is how to decentralize services by deploying digital infrastructure to facilitate such access. He said, "if I take the example of the government intranet, local communities have no access... we need to make it simple for citizens to access government services within their local communities". Mobile phones and radio may offer the means of extending e-governance services throughout the country especially in isolated rural areas or areas disadvantaged by the lack of adequate technological infrastructure.

ONLINE PRESENCE OF GOVERNMENT INSTITUTIONS

This section evaluates the extent of sophistication of government services on the Internet. Three forms of evaluation are discussed – the online presence of government ministries, local government institutions and politicians and political parties.

Online Presence of Government Ministries

A total of 14 websites of 16 government ministries were reviewed (November 2010). The websites of the ministries are outlined in Exhibit 27. Fourteen of the 16 websites of the ministries were found to be active (87.5%). The active websites included that of Ministry of Interior, Ministry of Foreign Affairs, Ministry of Justice and Ministry of Commerce. The online presence of a ministry is offers a means to inform citizens about the activities of the ministry and deliver a number of services such as downloading public documents (including activities ratios, reports, statistics, photos, maps, audio and video files).

The government tends to demonstrate a more transparent and open posture by ensuring the online presence of ministries is more than 50 per cent. These websites tend to be more informational with minimal or no interactive features.

Exhibit 27 Online Presence of Government Ministries

Name of Ministry	Website Address	Status	Phase (1, 2, 3, 4)
1. Ministère de l'intérieur	http://www.interieur.gouv.sn	Active	1
2. Ministère des affaires étrangères	http://www.diplomatie.gouv.sn	Active	1
3. Ministère de la justice	http://www.justice.gouv.sn	Active	1
4. Ministère du commerce	http://www.commerce.gouv.sn	Active	1
5. Ministère des forces armées	http://www.forcesarmees.gouv.sn	Inactive	1
6. Ministere de la jeunesse et des loisirs	http://www.jeunesse.gouv.sn	Active	1
7. Ministère de l'économie maritime	http://www.ecomaritime.gouv.sn	Active	1
8. Ministère de la sante et de la prévention	http://www.sante.gouv.sn	Active	1
9. Ministère de la culture, du genre et du cadre de vie	http://www.culture.gouv.sn	Active	1
10. Ministère de la famille et des organisations féminines	http://www.famille.gouv.sn	Inactive	1
11. Ministère de l'environnement et de la protection de la nature	http://www.environnement.gouv.sn	Active	1
12. Ministère de l'agriculture	http://www.agriculture.gouv.sn	Active	1
13. Ministère des mines, de l'industrie, de l'agro-industrie et des pme	http://www.industrie.gouv.sn	Active	1
14. Ministère de l'enseignement supérieur, des universités et des centres universitaires régionaux et de la recherche scientifique	http://www.recherche.gouv.sn	Active	1
15. Ministère de l'économie et des finances	http://www.finances.gouv.sn	Active	3
16. Direction générale de la comptabilité publique et du trésor (Ministère de l'économie et des finances)	http://www.tresor.gouv.sn	Active	1

Website Status (November 2011)
- Active – the website address works/opens and has content
- Inactive – the website address exists but there is no content or does not open
- None – there is no history of website development or website address does not exist

Phases of Digital Governance
- Phase 1 - Providing information (enabling information search)
- Phase 2 - Two way communication/Interactive (two-way communication services such as feedback forms, emails and bulletin boards)

Thirteen of the fourteen active websites reviewed are informative in nature and offer little room for interactivity between government (agencies) and citizens (see Exhibit 28 overleaf). Eleven of the fourteen websites provide public documents, reports and publications for download. The active websites are user-friendly and are maintained and updated regularly.

Exhibit 28 Review of 9 Active Government Websites

Review of 9 Active Government Websites	No. of Websites
Content	
The website provides current and accurate information	13
The website has public documents, reports and publications available for download	11
The website content is relevant and consistent with its objectives	13
Security/ Privacy	
The website has a privacy statement or information on confidentiality	4
The website uses an encryption method in collecting and processing citizens' information	1
Usability	
The website is easy to navigate and to find information and services - the items are well placed to enhance usability	13
Service	
The website provides adequate information to support decision-making and interaction with government	2
The website provides transactional services involving purchasing, paying of taxes, and requesting for information	1
Citizen Participation	
The website provides functionality for citizens to engage with government: discussions, forums, feedback/comments (very basic)	1
The website has social networking applications [Facebook, Twitter, google+, and RSS] to enhance interactivity	1

Four of the fourteen active websites provide a privacy statement or information on confidentiality. The website which tends to have some level of interactivity and transactional functionalities is the website of the Ministry of Economy and Finance. The website of the Ministry of Economy and Finance features functionality of electronic data exchange between different people who are authorized by a login and password. It also features a search engine, application syndication (RSS) and even a newsletter of the Directorate General of Public Accounting and the Treasury. Some websites, though being active have inadequate information. The Ministry of Foreign Affairs, for example, has a single page whilst all other pages are empty or at least do not have any contents displayed. The inactive websites are that of Ministry of Armed Forces and Ministry of Family and Women's organizations. The website of the Ministry of Armed Forces does not appear and warns that 'access to the server is not allowed'.

A number of websites (5) contain discussion forums, but they tend to be a "white elephant' – just an additional functionality - because there is no organized forum online. For a majority of the websites (13), there is also no integration with any web 2.0

functionalities like Facebook, and Twitter. Citizen interaction is limited to the download of forms on government services. This may be related to two factors: the technology being used is outdated and do not integrate these emerging Web 2.0 tools or developers choose not to use these functions in those sites, especially since these functionality may not be captured in their contractual terms-of-reference or job responsibilities. Given the technological developments that now allow to update the content or easily migrate to new versions of old software, it is reasonable to give more credence to the second hypothesis that the lack of networking tools social choice is deliberate on the part of designers the website portals.

However, according to the Coordinator of the ICT cluster and the Teleservices Accelerated Growth Strategy (AGS), this is due to the fact that

> "we are still in the first stage of dynamic websites, but the development of remote procedures, back-office applications are very important. Future website designs should include interactive applications to facilitate interaction between users and citizens".

The challenges in managing the websites of ministries lies in the accuracy and quality of information presented. An ICT consultant noted that ministerial reshuffle which are very common, have a negative effect on the quality of information brought online. Indeed, some sites still refer to ministries that were dissolved or converted long ago. These websites also face the challenge of enabling greater interactivity with users (integration of social networking applications). A governance expert purported that, "These sites provide information, but do not have any means of receiving feedback. What prevents the government and its departments, to develop forums through their websites?" Such feature could allow citizens and experts to comment and discuss the projects initiated by the government.

Further, while some sites of ministries do not work properly or are sometimes inaccessible, the website of the Ministry of Health and Prevention differs in many aspects. Redesigned for the third time in 2010, this site currently has important functions in operation: useful information, directories of online ministry, useful links, health statistics, multiple languages, et cetera. At its official launch in August 2010, the Ministry ensured that all the important statements and information are accessible via the website. The website was developed to provide different users (the general public, health professionals and, development partners) reliable information that can be used in their work and in decision making. The portal seems particularly well-visited by Internet users. Analyzing the statistics of the new portal, the webmaster noted that the website has progressively increased its visitors between June and August 2010. Within the three months, 72,071 visitors have browsed this site with an average 326 visitors a day. The statistics also reveal that the portal 29.7% of website visitors were interested in the link of the National Education Information for Health (SENEPS) while 14.5% of website visitors consult the News section and 14.2% consulted publications on health care.

Online Presence of Government Agencies and Local Government Institutions

Websites implemented by local authorities differ largely from those developed by government bodies (see Exhibit 29 overleaf). Some of them are equipped with social networking tools so that these features are absent from the type of gate proposed by the ministries. For this reason, one governance expert shared that there is a trend that is about to happen. To illustrate his point of view, he argues that

> "in seeing the site of the mayor of Gorée and also the site of the current mayor of Dakar I visit often, I find there is progress in terms of participation. The opportunity is given to citizens of the city of Dakar to communicate, to comment on the various activities that lead to the level of the city of Dakar, private companies also can view the offers. Therefore, there is an involvement of the people in the life of the community and I think all towns should move in that direction".

On some websites (such as that of the City Council of Kaffrine) the ability to create a personal space accessible by login and password. Users can also access public documents such as tenders available for download. The information provided by these sites is not updated frequently. According to the former Technical Advisor to the Minister of ICT, these similarities are the fact that

> "the challenges of the Senegalese administration generally in the field of ICT are similar to the challenges of local communities. There is no policy which is formulated at the central level with clear objectives for local communities. So we are left with either local authorities who have outdated websites or local communities that simply do not have sites. On the other hand, those with websites haves no program of development and use of ICT to enhance the potential regional or local ones".

The SIP-type websites have long been the template for each local authority as a criteria to join the group of "connected cities". They were designed using a participatory methodology involving the local youth in the collection of information.

Exhibit 29 Online Presence of Selected Government Agencies and Local Government Institutions

Name of Government Agency and Local Government Institution	Website Address	Status	Phase (1, 2, 3, 4)
1. Mairie de ville de Dakar	http://www.villededakar.org	Active	1
2. Mairie de ville de Rufisque	http://www.mairiederufisque.org	Active	1
3. Mairie de ville de Saint Louis	http://www.villedesaintlouis.com	Active	1
4. Mairie de la ville de Matam	http://sipsenegal.org/matam	Active	1
5. Mairie de la Commune d'arrondissement de Dakar Plateau	http://dakarplateau.org	Active	1
6. Mairie de la Commune d'arrondissement de Gorée	http://www.mairiedegoree.org	Active	1
7. Mairie de ville de Kaffrine	http://www.kaffrine.org	Active	2
8. Mairie de la ville de Tambacounda	http://mairietambacounda.com	Active	1
9. Mairie de la Commune de Dagana	http://www.dagana.net	Active	1
10. Mairie de la Commune de Kébémer	http://www.sipsenegal.org/kebemer	Active	1
11. Mairie de la Commune d'arrondissement de Médina	http://www.medinacite.sn	Inactive	1
12. Mairie de la Commune d'arrondissement des Parcelles Assainies	http://www.parcellesassainies.org	Active	1
13. Mairie de la Commune de Gandiaye	http://www.sipsenegal.org/gandiaye	Active	1
14. Mairie de la Commune d'arrondissement de Yoff	http://www.mairieyoff.org	Active	1
15. Mairie de la Commune d'arrondissement de Ngor	http://www.communedengor.sn	Active	1
16. Mairie de la Commune d'arrondissement de Grand Dakar	http://www.mairiegrandakar.com	Inactive	1
17. Mairie de la Commune de Koungheul	http://www.koungheul.org	Active	1

Website Status (November 2011)
- Active – the website address works/opens and has content
- Inactive – the website address exists but there is no content or does not open
- None – there is no history of website development or website address does not exist

Phases of Digital Governance
- Phase 1 - Providing information (enabling information search)
- Phase 2 - Two way communication/Interactive (two-way communication services such as feedback forms, email and bulletin boards)
- Phase 3 - Transaction services (facilitating transaction services for businesses and citizens)
- Phase 4 - Transforming process (transforming services from government to the citizens e.g. e-voting or opinion poll).

The websites promote the awareness of the importance of ICT in the management of local authorities in Senegal. However, given the gaps in their design and maintenance (uniform presentation and update problems); they have been gradually overtaken by the new websites of cities that clearly demonstrate the desire to move towards more interactive applications.

Another major challenge is linking or integrating local authorities to a number of website addresses which have been made inactive. Depending on the changes taking place in the leadership of a local authority, local authorities tend to have several successive websites. Each municipal team is indeed interested primarily in new achievements and a trend away from anything that can be recognized as an asset of the outgoing team. The most notable example is the District Municipality of Medina who had successively developed three websites over a period of 10 years. In 1997, the mayor was given a project website by the Information Systems People (www.sip.sn/Medina). In 2007, the mayor launched a new portal (www.medinacite.sn) before returning quickly to the new version of SIP addresses (http://sipsenegal.org/medina). The major drawback with these changes is that they create confusion among users already familiar with the old addresses.

According to experts, the existence or disappearance of certain municipal websites may be linked to two main factors: (i) political instability or the periodic change of leadership, and (ii) the unwillingness of the new head of the town hall to consolidate the gains made by predecessors. As a result, between 1997 and 2010, many municipal websites have collapsed. It is therefore important to educate stakeholders in the interest of continuity of service by continuing achievements that may lead to the establishment of effective e-governance.

Experts believe that e-governance projects studied are facing serious managerial deficiencies related to: (i) the lack of human resources, (ii) the limited material and financial resources, (iii) the unwillingness of politicians, and (iv) the disinterestedness of their fellow citizens. These shortcomings lead to several consequences; the most noticeable are the absence of widespread networking and public sites created, the lack of internet connection in town halls and the low operating potential of ICT in general. In such contexts, the initiatives rarely give the desired results. Finally, it is important to increase the number of local authorities that have a websites. Their websites should go beyond simply providing information about the life and activities of the community, to making visitors aware of appropriate digital tools in governance.

Exhibit 30 Online Presence of Political Parties and Selected Politicians

	Name of Political Party	Website Address	Status	Phase (1, 2, 3, 4)
1.	Alliance des Forces de Progrès (AFP)	http://www.afp-senegal.org	Active	1
2.	Parti Socialiste (PS)	http://www.ps-senegal.com	Active	1
3.	Alliance Jef Jel (AJJ)	http://www.alliancejefjel.org	Active	1
4.	Parti de l'Indépendance et du Travail (PIT)	http://www.pit-senegal.com	Inactive	NA
5.	Taxaw Temm (Ibrahima Fall)	http://www.ibrahimafall.com	Active	1
6.	Ligue Démocratique/Mouvement pour le Parti du Travail (LD/MPT)	http://www.ldmpt.sn	Active	1
7.	Union pour le Renouveau Démocratique (URD)	http://www.urdsenegal.sn	Inactive	NA
8.	And Jef / PADS (Parti Africain pour la Démocratie et le Socialisme)	http://andjefpads.centerblog.net	Active	1
Online Presence of Selected Politicans				
1.	Abdoulaye Wade	http://abdoulaye-wade.org http://www.facebook.com/pages/ABDOULAYE-WADE/182058165129	Active	1
2.	Ousmane Tanor Dieng	http://www.tanor-dieng.com http://fr-fr.facebook.com/pages/Ousmane-Tanor-Dieng/74004728550	Active	1
3.	Macky Sall	http://mackysall.centerblog.net http://www.facebook.com/pages/Macky-Sall-Officielle/214619238559688	Active	1
4.	Talla Sylla	http://tallasylla.wordpress.com http://fr-fr.facebook.com/people/Talla-Sylla/1009235236	Active	1

Website Status (November 2011)
- <u>Active</u> – the website address works/opens and has content
- <u>Inactive</u> – the website address exists but there is no content or does not open
- <u>None</u> – there is no history of website development or website address does not exist

Phases of Digital Governance
- <u>Phase 1</u> - Providing information (enabling information search)
- <u>Phase 2</u> - Two way communication/Interactive (two-way communication services such feedback forms, emails and bulletin boards)
- <u>Phase 3</u> - Transaction services (facilitating transaction services for businesses and citizens)
- <u>Phase 4</u> - Transforming process (transforming services from government to the citizens e.g. e-voting or opinion poll).

Online Presence of Politicians and Political Parties

Exhibit 30 (previous page) outline the online presence of political parties and selected politicians. The use of digital tools and in particular the Internet in politics offers a means for politicians to campaign and engage with the young electorate. As one politician puts it, the internet is "a requirement of modernity and political survival". Another city council official share that

"it is a good piece of political marketing full of reward. Today the electorate is an one that loves young so-called social networks. It is in the interest of the people to understand that this category of voters is connected all the time. Also, in the era of ICT, the politicians are creating more and more sites to try to popularize their image and make their own propaganda, it's interesting from them".

As an illustration, 216 comments were posted in response to 16 text messages on the Facebook page of Talla Sylla between October 5 and November 3, 2011, or on a one-month period. Discussion topics are varied but the central theme relates to politics: it is criticism against the government, personal political project ideas, and expressions of sympathy for fellow party members, or opinions on current national and international politics. However, not all Facebook friends belong to the electorate or eligible voters in the country. Hence, these exchanges do not measure the actual influence of the politician in the politics.

On the other hand, some citizens have a different view on politicians' use of digital tools and the Internet. Some citizens consider the use of these digital tools by politicians as a reactive strategy to contemporary trends in communication. As a result, there is no adequate or strategic assessment underpinning the development or use of the website. These websites tend to have very little useful or relevant information for the public, and are poorly managed or updated. For example, the website of the Independence Party and Labour (PIT) was last updated in 2006. These websites seldom have public documents available for download; they are designed to promote partisan objectives.

E-GOVERNANCE IMPACT

E-governance and National Development

Experts believe that in general e-governance initiatives can support national development if used appropriately. There are two positive contributions to consider. First, these projects can strengthen democracy and transparency of government business to the public, and, second, allow businesses to access government procurement processes. Concerning the latter, ORBUS Branch of Customs is an online clearance system that allows a reduction of customs processing while eliminating travel related to these efforts. The system introduces greater efficiency in the provision of clearance services and facilitates phasing out the use of paper. The potential of e-governance to support national development is seen in: (i) the efficiency of service delivery, (ii) speed, traceability and transparency of procedures, and (iii) the participation of citizens in governance. However, it appears that these potential effects are more theoretical and are less observable in practice. With the exception of the availability of information online constantly, most of the positive effects described are more related to the perception of that experience. There are other challenges which mitigate the potential benefits to be obtained from e-governance, namely: (i) ignorance of initiatives by citizens, (ii) the low level of education of the population, and (ii) the high cost of technical infrastructure.

Most importantly, it is important to inform the public, raise awareness about the opportunities of e-governance and adapt to their needs and achievements. This could be done through an extensive advertising campaign across TV, radio and print media. It is also important to create public access points to the Internet using licensed facilitators to provide access to the illiterate.

E-governance and the MDGs

The investigation revealed the existence of a relationship between the experiences of e-governance and the achievement of the Millennium Development Goals (MDGs), although the experts have difficulty in demonstrating the relationship in the case of Senegal. In the view of a governance expert,

> "e-governance applies to all sectors and, therefore, has an effect on the Millennium Development Goals that relate to various sectors including health and gender development".

According to the coordinator of the ICT Cluster teleservice and the Accelerated Growth Strategy (AGS), appropriate electronic applications can be used to raise awareness of the dangers inherent in practices such as female genital mutilation, and the encirclement of certain areas that cannot have access to education. The former adviser to the Minister of ICT perceives the role of ICT in two ways:

> "they provide information, first, to identify the challenges of development, and second, to define appropriate policies to address these challenges".

The first order of positive effects is related to the optimization of the quality of information and public service. According to experts interviewed, the development of e-government is a guarantee of the availability of information and implementation of automated administrative procedures. The second order of the positive effects of e-governance is related to the opportunities associated with online procedures. There have been advances in education – through mobile text messaging, parents and students have real-time access to national examination results. Further, though marginal, telemedicine is beginning to be a reality. The third level of perception of positive effects of e-governance is the reduction of the duration of the procedures hence time savings. Online access to public services facilitates the reduction of corrupt practices associated with the delivery of public services.

E-governance and Principles of Democracy

According to experts, e-governance initiatives in principle promote democracy and good governance if it is from the citizen-centric perspective. Within this perspective, the optimization of the quality of public services, citizen participation and the promotion of transparency remain critical goals for the establishment of democracy and good governance. For this reason, experts believe that e-governance projects have a major role in that they offer several advantages: (i) improving the organization of the internal procedures of governments, (ii) availability of better information and better services, (iii) increasing the transparency of management and reduced corruption, (iv) strengthening the credibility of institutions and the responsibility of administrative officials, and (v) development of new practices of participation and consultation for the public. According to one expert interviewed, these benefits are real because

> "now in Guédiawaye all deliberations of the council are accessible via the Internet; simply log on and enter our portal. You stand right behind your computer on any search engine to view the proceedings. It has never existed before and this became a reality today, suddenly creating democracy through transparency and information sharing in real time".

Ensuring transparency promotes confidence among citizens on governance processes.

E-governance and Local Government Administration

Expert opinions are divided on this issue. According to some, the website of the local community allows the elected local officers to communicate their mission, achievements and the constraints being faced by the community. In return, the portal provides an opportunity for citizens to challenge the rulers about their activities. This is, according to one expert, is "a form of remote control of politics at the local level". Concrete examples were popularized with the project, Information Systems Popular (SIP), which had led to the first generation of municipal websites. Other examples include the digitization of cadastral offered by organizations such as Manobi Senegal, and the introduction of software for management and accounting in municipalities and rural communities. Most of these applications had proven effects on the organizational and delivery of local government.

Without denying these benefits, an e-governance consultant expressed some reservations on the grounds that the full potential offered by ICTs for local governance is not fully exploited, particularly in terms of facilitating the flow of information. The expert goes on that

"such information could be provided by a series of intermediaries that are in development organizations at the base (CBOs, NGOs) who are opinion leaders within communities".

Another expert commented that "these initiatives have no remarkable effects in the functioning of local governments to the extent that it is the preserve of experts".

This is also the opinion of another expert who seems to regret the fact that "local authorities have just the tool".

Most websites of local governments tend to meet two needs related to regional marketing and political patronage. Strategies that support them are based essentially on: (i) the "territorial marketing" proceeding from the will of elected officials to promote the image of their city on the international scene, (ii) the "political proselytism" which involves the exhibition of the achievements of the municipal team, in order to gain the trust of voters wooed incessantly, and (iii) making available new services administered online or "e-government." In any case, the dialogue with the people, promotion of local development and the achievement of a quality public service are not actually incorporated in the objectives for developing these websites.

E-governance and Citizen Empowerment

The opinions of experts differ on the link between e-governance and citizen empowerment. Some experts believe that the effectiveness of e-governance projects is evident through experiments such as "administrative line". However, it is obvious that this site neither provides specific information on procedures nor allows citizens to effectively engage in fruitful exchanges with the leaders. Thus, the potential benefits of these applications include: (i) the reduction in waiting times for public service users to access services (information) provided to them by government, (ii) reduced travel and additional costs and other risks that must be endured by the users of public services, and (iii) strengthening the links between state officials and citizens through greater confidence in public service delivery. However, other experts suggest a more critical review on the fact that the provision of information online is not enough to ensure citizen engagement with government bodies. Although ministries have websites, there are many problems that stem from the content being limited to the presentation of the institution and its missions. These websites are much more like a storefront advertising and a medium of communication and exchange on the aspirations of the national population. As one expert puts it

> "normally, if the citizen has information online, it does not need to move into administrative services. In this case, these initiatives may allow the participation of citizens, if asked by the government. But this is not the case in Senegal".

While governance requires the participation of grassroots communities to ensure the effectiveness of governance, it must be said that there is still much to do in the context of e-governance initiatives launched in Senegal. Given the difficulties of mobility in Dakar and in other parts of the country, these projects could have an obvious impact on how citizens interact with government. The website may indeed be a forum for communication and dialogue where everyone can give their views and exercise control over the action of the central or local government. However, only a few people, including elected officials, are aware of the existence of the website in their community. Therefore, the level of citizen participation remains very low.

E-governance and Environmental Protection/Climate Change

Experts generally argue that the link between the initiatives of e-governance and environmental protection and climate change is not obvious or at least the impact of these experiences on the environment is not visible. There are also no plans specifically formulated with the aim to manage environmental problems through the use of e-governance applications. This justifies the response of the former adviser of the Minister of ICT who sees, "...the relationship but not in the case of Senegal, where there are no public policies or programs on ICT effectively to climate change". Some respondents, however, consider an indirect relationship due to the fact that some centres of expertise on the environment, particularly the Ecological Monitoring Centre (SSC) have begun to contribute digital tools to make predictions and reduce the impacts of potential disasters that could adversely affect the natural resource management.

Another example is illustrative of the potential impact of the experiences of e-governance on the environment due to the benefits accrued from reduced travel. A governance expert explained that

> "organizing virtual meetings reduced consumer spending and hydrocarbon emissions into the atmosphere. However, the use of electronics also generates CO_2 which would impair the quality of the environment".

The availability and flow of information is probably decisive evidence on which experts base the justification of the digital input to environmental management. One expert explained that issues related to climate change can be considered and addressed through initiatives using ICTs at national and local levels. He argues that there are many uses to which technologies could be put, including natural disasters and early-warning systems. While ICTs could be used for data collection particularly in areas affected by sea erosion, GPS technologies could be also be leveraged to monitor environmental changes in communities. There is also the potential to create community awareness of any impending disaster.

E-governance and Inter-Agency Collaboration

The effects of e-governance initiatives on the organizational structure and functioning of government institutions, including how they share information with each other, are not shown explicitly. Within an administration, it is possible to identify positive impacts. Giving the example of the management system of public finances, one public sector official states that "is a system that now enables all stakeholders to share the database of all public expenditures already incurred, those not executed, and those in liquidation. Previously we needed to move or at least to visit this or that person to find information; now, when you access the system you have access to all information in place". The most popular inter-agency initiative is the government intranet. Seen as the first step towards the "e-government" in Senegal, this network provides the State with a modern infrastructure and efficient communication. It has several advantages. In addition to being designed on open-source software, the application provides communication facilities, technical and financial benefits. For example, IP telephony implementation in this framework provides officials an opportunity to communicate with each other without restriction and without charge. It also helps to reduce the telephone bill of the administration, and deployment of teleconferencing, and directory services.

In reference to the statistics from ADIE, the phone budget of the state is estimated at 8 billion CFA francs[1]. There are also the likely benefits of reduced consumption of paper, especially now that a legal framework has been designed to give validity to electronic documents[2]. The challenge now is to popularize the tool and its widespread use in all national public services. Indeed, despite the funding of the extension phase of the intranet since 2008 and the announcement by the authorities to cover the entire country by June 2009 [3], many administrative services located in several parts of the country still have no access to the government intranet. One of the major factors that explain this situation is that government spending are essentially confined within the capital and some major cities such as Thies, Saint Louis and Diourbel. The gap is evident between the declarations of intent and the implementation of commitments.

---

[1] ADIE, *Fiche Projet Intranet Gouvernemental,* Dakar, 2007.
[2] République du Sénégal, *Loi n 2008 – 10 portant loi d'orientation relative à la société de l'information*, Dakar, le 25 janvier 2008.

[3] Agence de Presse Sénégalaise, « Abdoulaye Baldé lance le programme intranet administratif », mercredi 21 mai2008.

GAPS TO BE ADDRESSED

Two key gaps – e-readiness and education and training – are discussed in this section.

E-readiness

There is a need for appropriate assessment of the Senegal's readiness to take advantage of new and emerging technologies for good governance. One expert contends that "these initiatives are appropriate and should be strengthened and grown". Further, it is useful to note that these projects are initiated under the seal of a digital revolution without prior consideration of the need to design strategies to bring the projects to fruition. . The vision of e-Senegal is an example that envisages a double transition ("e-government" and "e-citizen") without interest in the preconditions for implementation, particularly with regards to ICT access and literacy of the masses. Thus, current e-governance initiatives lack reference to the realities of the national context. There tends to be a gap between the objectives of e-governance at the national level and realities of implementation at level of local governments. Factors which affect the e-readiness to implement e-governance initiatives include the limited capital resources dedicated to them.

Experts argue that the country is facing budgetary constraints causing the prioritisation of other sectors. E-governance projects do require considerable financial resources. Thus the current appearance that the Senegalese government does not devote sufficient resources to fund the technological leap required for the implementation of e-administration is a hindrance. Financial readiness has also influenced the development of access infrastructure whose costs are prohibitive for the majority of the Senegalese population. On the other hand, the deficiencies in policies and programmes in e-governance in Senegal are numerous. Experts shared three key gaps in policies and programmes:

> (i) interoperability of applications between government agencies, (ii) expanding access to internet, especially within rural communities, and (iii)availability of requisite human resources who have strategic understanding of both the technical and social dimensions of digital tools to be deployed in the country.

Other factors which affect the development of policies and practices of e-governance in Senegal are as follows:

1. Limited access to e-governance applications resulting from (i) connectivity problems, (ii) the lack of infrastructure, (iii) lack of competence by officers and citizens on ICT, (iv) illiteracy, and (v) insufficient financial resources for the promotion of e-governance.

2. Poor objectives of e-governance initiatives: it includes (i) the inadequacy of systems with the level of understanding of citizens, (ii) focusing on the Internet at the expense of mobile solutions, (iii) the significance of external financing, (iv) the absence of automated services, (v) the lack of communication and awareness of citizens on the opportunities offered by e-governance applications, (vi) the non-involvement of people in the policy and programme development, and (vii) lack of performance evaluation of e-governance projects in conjunction with the needs expressed by the people.

However, it seems that technology is not the most important factor in e-governance projects. In the opinion of an expert interviewed, "a successful project needs a good policy and not just a good technology". For example, the Senegalese culture is dominated by orality that facilitates ownership of mobile phones by almost all segments of population. According to statistics released by the Observatory of the Regulatory Agency for Telecommunications and Posts (ARTP), four out of five Senegalese now have a mobile phone. E-readiness assessment could emphasise the need to adopt low-cost technologies for e-governance initiatives.

Education and Training

Assuming that Senegal already has a good technological infrastructure, the experts emphasized the need to focus on education and training of citizens. "Before rendering services to citizens, we still need the service to be truly available and interfaced well, but this is not necessarily the case for the moment", one expert intimated. While state agencies are still yet to deploy applications, it seems necessary to increase the levels of equipment and access points to broadband both in the cities and rural communities to close the digital divide. There are obviously a number of efforts required to achieve effective participation of citizens. In view of suggestions made by experts, four areas of action need to be explored:

(i) community involvement in finding solutions tailored to their needs, (ii) raising public awareness about the role they can play in the governance of their community, (iii) capacity building to facilitate their participation, and (iv) development of the incentives based on the premise that an act done electronically should be cheaper than its traditional form.

The integration of issues related to e-governance, e-government and e-democracy in the curricula of university education is really a crucial question that academics interviewed have given much attention to. This integration must necessarily pass through a preliminary analysis of the current educational gaps in supporting e-governance. This assessment may allow the development of training modules which are consistent with the needs of the nation and the skills of the citizens. Computer training schools could also be a good lever for change if people who are trained in software development are encouraged to reflect on the types of e-governance applications to offer, through mobile phones, citizens and local authorities. The process of implementation of such a project needs to be based on a clear structured around concrete objectives that support, in an academic setting, the real problems that exist in government and other organizations. It should be supported by a political commitment to undertake a review of educational programs that will be updated taking into account current developments in the information society.

Practice Question 17

1. What is the relationship between e-governance policies and strategic programmes to implement e-governance policies?

....

....

....

....

....

....

....

....

....

....

....

....
....
....
....
....
....
....
....
....
....
....
....
....
....
....
....
....
....
....

2. How did Senegal ensure a strategic fit between the policies and strategic programmes and activities?

....

....

....

....

....

....

....

....

....

....

....

....

....

....

....

....

....

....

....

....

....

....

....

....

....

....

....

....

....

....

....

....

....

....

....

....

3. What is the relationship between e-governance policies, programmes and the online activities of government ministries and local government agencies.

....

....

....

....

....

....

....

....

....

....

....

....

....

....

....

....

....

....

....

....

....

....

....

....

....

....

....

....

....

....

....

....

....

....

....

....

4. What are key challenges to the implementation of e-governance policies in Senegal?

....

....

....

....

....

....

....

....

....

....

....

....

....

....

....

....

....

....

....

....

....

....

....

....

....

....

....

....

....

....

....

....

....

....

....

5. Has e-governance policies and strategic programmes being successful in achieving e-governance objectives in Senegal?

....

....

....

....

....

....

....

....

....

....

....

....

....

....

....

....

....

....

....

....

....

....

....

....

....

....

....

....

....

....

....

....

....

....

....

....

....

....

CHAPTER SUMMARY

The chapter explored the link between policies (e-governance) to strategic programmes to implement the policies. This was done through a case study on e-governance in Senegal. The components covered were e-governance objectives and goals, e-governance policies, e-governance programmes and projects/initiatives, online presence of government institutions, impact of e-governance and gaps to be addressed. The gaps to be addressed refer to the need to revise the national ICT policies or related policies which tend to stipulate e-governance objectives. In Senegal, there tends to be an apparent disconnect between e-governance objectives at national level and realities of implementation at level of local government. As a result, an e-readiness assessment may be required to make e-governance objectives and implementation strategies more contextually relevant. There is also the need for interoperability of applications between government agencies, need to improve Internet accessibility, need to improve access to e-governance applications (local content in local languages), periodic performance evaluation of e-governance applications, need for education and training of citizens and need for low-cost technologies like mobiles for e-governance initiatives.

In effect, we learn that policy implementation is complex and usually constrained by the lack of resources.

Chapter 7 – Strategic Management Theories

The objective of this chapter is to introduce students to two theories used in analyzing the strategic behavior or decisions of firms. These theories - Resource-Based Theory (RBT) and Dynamic Capabilities (DC) Framework - have received much attention in strategic management and business studies, and are relevant in examining the strategic behavior of firms.

DEFINING THEORY

The definition of theory can be taken from different perspectives, depending on the objective of the definition. In terms of its consistent elements or components, a theory can be conceptualized as

> "a system of constructs and propositions that conjointly demonstrates a logical and yet systematic and coherent account of a phenomenon bounded by some assumptions and conditions" (Bacharach, 1989).

On the other hand, in terms of its purpose, a theory can also be viewed as a

> "coherent set of general propositions used as principles of explanation, understanding and/or prediction of the apparent relationships of certain observed phenomena" (Zikmund, 2003). A theory has been empirically tested and verified and can be shown as a schematic diagram, mathematical equation and words.

In its essence, a theory presents a way of studying concepts or variables concerning a phenomenon in order to find or investigate the solution for a research problem. A theory also explains or predicts occurrences by outlining the relationships between concepts or variables which underpin a phenomenon. However, to offer explanations or predictions, theories tend to possess certain characteristics. These characteristics, espoused by academics (Gregor, 2006; Bhattacherjee, 2012), include:

Theory is not data, facts, typologies, taxonomies or empirical findings. Theories are not an ad hoc collection of constructs without relationships; they must have propositions (relationships), explanations, and boundary conditions.

The explanations offered by theories are nomothetic. Thus, they tend to go beyond explaining single events to offer explanations which are generalizable across situations, events, or people. As such, they are less precise, less complete and tend to focus on patterns of events, behavior or phenomena.

Theories operate at a conceptual level and stem from logic; however, data and findings operate at the empirical or observational level.

For a theory to be well understood, there are some foundational premises that need to be set. These are constructs, propositions, logic, and boundary conditions or assumptions (Bhattacherjee, 2012). The constructs of a theory define what the theory is about and also explain what concepts are important for understanding a phenomenon. Propositions, on the other hand, are about how these concepts are related to each other. The logic of a theory explains why the concepts are related and the boundary conditions or assumptions probe the "who, when, and where" by bringing out the circumstances under which these concepts and relationships work.

For the purposes of the case studies in this book, two theories are presented in this section. These theories have received much attention in strategic management and business studies, and are relevant in examining the strategic behavior of firms.

RESOURCE-BASED THEORY (RBT)

Defining Resources: Assets and Capabilities

RBT tends to be the prevailing paradigm that explains or helps to understand how and why firms develop the capability to gain and sustain competitive advantage (Penrose, 1995; Wernerfelt, 1984; Barney, 1991). Its later extension, the dynamic capabilities approach examines how these firms adapt and even capitalize on rapidly changing technological or volatile environments as in DCs (Teece *et al.,* 1997). Within these theoretical frameworks, rival firms are viewed to compete on the basis of their internal characteristics, resources, through which they build competitive advantage and a superior long-term performance (Wernerfelt, 1984; Barney, 1991; Wade & Hulland, 2004).

Traditional strategic analysis considers a firm's resources as strengths that a firm uses *to conceive of and implement their strategies* (Learned *et al.*, 1969; Porter, 1981). These strengths include 'all assets, capabilities, organizational processes, firm attributes, information, knowledge, et cetera controlled by a firm that enable the firm to conceive of and implement strategies which improve its efficiency and effectiveness' (Daft, 1983 cited in Barney, 1991: 101). This seemingly broader perspective of firm resources has been recently narrowed as 'assets and capabilities that are available and useful in detecting and responding to market opportunities' (Sanchez *et al.*, 1996 and Christensen & Overdorf, 2000 cited in Wade & Hulland, 2004: 109). Assets are considered as anything tangible or intangible which a firm uses in 'its processes for creating, producing, and/or offering its products (goods or services) to a market, whereas capabilities are repeatable patterns of actions in the use of assets to create, produce, and/or offer products to a market' (Sanchez *et al.*, 1996 cited in Wade & Hulland, 2004: 109). Other authors who tend to differentiate resources from capabilities; define resources as tangible or intangible assets or inputs to production, and capabilities as a *coordinated set of tasks* which utilize these assets for the purpose of achieving a particular end result. Both conceptualizations, however, agree that capabilities utilize assets to achieve a defined organizational objective.

Assets can be classified as tangible, intangible and personnel-based resources (Grant, 1991). Tangible assets include 'the financial capital and the physical assets of the firm such as plant, equipment, and stocks of raw materials'; intangible assets comprise 'assets such as reputation, brand image and product quality'; and personnel-based (or organizational) assets include technical know-how, managerial commitment, knowledge and skills, organizational culture, employee training and loyalty (Bharadwaj, 2000: 171).

Assets are assembled, integrated and deployed within business processes to form the capabilities which an organization uses to improve its efficiency and effectiveness (Grant, 1991).

In a broader conceptualization, an organizational capability is 'a high-level routine (or collection of routines) that together with its implementing input flows, confer upon the organization's management a set of decision options for producing significant outputs of particular type' (Winter, 2000 cited in Winter, 2003: 991). This collection of routines can also be considered as being operational or dynamic depending on their ability to cause change (rates of change) or impact through their output in the organization. Operational or ordinary capabilities, also known as ordinary or 'zero-level' capabilities are 'those that permit a firm to 'make a living' in the short-term', while dynamic capabilities, are those that 'operate to extend, modify or create ordinary capabilities' (Winter, 2003: 991). Dynamic capabilities, from the dynamic capabilities approach (Teece *et al.,* 1997) is 'an extension of the resource-based view of the firm that was introduced to explain how firms can develop their capability to adapt and even capitalize on rapidly changing technological environments' (Montealegre, 2002: 516). They are developed through the appropriate adaptation, integration, and reconfiguration of internal and external organizational assets, capabilities and business processes to respond to the dynamic business environment (Teece *et al.,* 1997).

On the other hand, recent work by Wang & Ahmed (2007), in building on this conceptualization of capabilities, further explains that 'dynamic capabilities are the 'ultimate' organizational capabilities that are conducive to long-term performance, rather than simply a 'subset' of the capabilities, as Teece *et al.* (1997) suggest' (p. 36). The authors conceptualize capabilities in three classifications: capabilities (first order), core capabilities (second-order), and dynamic capabilities (third order). In their argument, firms deploy operational or ordinary capabilities to attain a desired goal which ensures their economic survival. Core capabilities are deployed when a bundle of resources are deployed in the strategic direction of the firm. Dynamic capabilities become the overarching capabilities which go beyond achieving economic survival and strategic objectives to ensure that a firm's performance is sustained in response to the threats and opportunities in its business environment. They enable a firm to develop core capabilities among other resources and deploy them to create and sustain a strategic advantage in its business environment. This makes them critical to a firm's performance in rapidly changing technological environments (Teece *et al.,* 1997) and the volatile environments in DCs (Okoli & Mbarika, 2003). This transformation of resources occurs in a 'swift, precise and creative manner' in line with the threats and changes to its strategic orientation (Wang

& Ahmed, 2007: 36).

A capability may therefore exist as an ordinary capability until it is deployed alongside other resources in the strategic orientation of the firm to become a core capability or address an environmental change and/or to sustain firm performance to become a dynamic capability. This also presupposes that the creative potential of these capabilities, or in broader perspective, resources, differs. One may then ask what makes these resources differ in their ability to enable a firm to create and sustain its performance in the marketplace. This leads us to consider the attributes of resources.

Resource Attributes

RBT posits that to create and sustain a competitive advantage or achieve a performance beyond that of its competitors in the marketplace, a firm's resources must be *heterogeneous* and *immobile*, and to have that potential, the resources must simultaneously have attributes of being valuable, rare, imperfectly imitable and not strategically substitutable or non-substitutable by other resources (Barney, 1991) – the VRIN conditions (Bowman & Ambrosini, 2003). The attributes are briefly explained as follows:

Valuable: For a firm's resource to be valuable, it must be able to help the organization conceive of and implement strategies capable of exploiting opportunities and neutralizing threats in its environment and thereby improve its efficiency and effectiveness (Barney, 1991). It must be able to generate rents - lower costs in delivering products than that of competitors or revenue from differentiating its products (goods or services) - to be captured by the firm (Bowman & Ambrosini, 2000). The resource remains appropriate for the rent generating activity when the costs of exploiting the resource do not offset the rents generated (Peteraf, 1993). For example, in the development of a new product in a manufacturing firm, the cost of exploiting a resource should not be more than the profits made from the new product; otherwise the value creation process becomes relatively unsustainable with time.

Rare: To create an organizational performance beyond economic survival, a resource has to be rare, uncommon or scarce in its distribution across the competitors in the market (Amit & Schoemaker, 1993). It should be rare in its functionality and not just its type – functionality lies in capabilities generated from a combination of resources such as tangible, intangible and organizational assets (Bharadwaj, 2000: 171). The lack of rare resources creates competitive parity, where no firm obtains a clear competitive advantage, but 'firms do increase their ability of economic survival' (Porter, 1980 cited in Barney, 1991: 107). Some types of resources like IT infrastructure are easily available on the market, however, when combined with other organizational resources like managerial skills and knowledge, organizations can create a functionality - market responsiveness or customer support capability - which may be rare across the competitors in the market (Santhanam & Hartono, 2003).

Imperfect Imitability. Resources become imperfectly imitable when it is more difficult for competing firms to replicate them (Bowman & Ambrosini, 2003: 291). These occur in the presence of isolating mechanisms (Rumelt, 1984); when, firstly, its occurrence or availability to the organization is due to its unique historical conditions; secondly, the link between resources and the firm's sustained competitive advantage is causally ambiguous, and lastly, resources themselves are socially complex in nature (Dierickx & Cool, 1989; Barney, 1991). These isolating mechanisms increase the costs of competing firms in imitating a successful firm's resources. When other competitors imitate a functionality or are able to obtain other resources capable of substituting that resource, the resource loses its ability to create a sustained competitive advantage or organizational performance, though it may be valuable to the organization and rare among rival firms. It thus becomes important for resources to be also imperfectly imitable, and beyond that, become not strategically substitutable by other resources.

Non-Substitutability. Substitutes can be in the form of imitating resources exactly or using different resources to create the effect of a resource as used in the successful firms. Competing firms are able to develop substitutes when they are able to discern the value-creation process and understand the value contributed by the resource possessed by the successful firm (Barney, 1991: 292). These substitutes are only valuable when competing firms are able to achieve a low-cost strategy for developing and exploiting the resource to achieve a value same as or superior to that of the successful firm. However, in the presence of the isolating mechanisms discussed earlier, discerning or understanding the value creation process of resources becomes difficult. This increases the costs of imitation and substitution, reducing the value or rents generated by the substitutes (Bowman & Ambrosini, 2003: 292).

In effect, RBT states that creating competitive advantage lies in the heterogeneity of valuable resources or in possessing resources that are valuable, appropriate and rare or uncommon across firms, and sustaining that advantage depends on them being imperfectly mobile; inimitable and non-substitutable (Barney, 1991; Wade & Hulland, 2004: 117-118). So then how does the concept of ordinary, core and dynamic capabilities fit in?

As earlier explained, dynamic capabilities go beyond ensuring the company's economic survival to enabling it to sustain and achieve new benefits thereby sustaining and improving its performance. Economic survival occurs when a company tends to have just valuable resources that enable it to obtain competitive parity. At this stage the resources may consist of largely ordinary capabilities, and perhaps a few core capabilities. However, the need to go beyond economic survival is arguably typical of the idiosyncratic institutional uncertainties in DCs (Okoli & Mbarika, 2003). Any change necessitating the detailed customization of the product, integration with other products, or extension of its functionalities to serve a specific or different target market requires the combination and reconfiguration of organizational assets and capabilities in order to achieve and sustain new benefits thereby sustaining and improving its performance (Winter, 2003: 991). In other scenarios such as the case of merger or acquisition at the firm-level or new developments in the national ICT infrastructure, a firm may expand its resource portfolio.

However, without deploying the new resources in, perhaps, the 'redefined' strategic direction of the firm, the rent generating ability of the new resources acquired may not be fully exploited. The firm may therefore need to develop higher order capabilities – core and dynamic – which extend the functionalities of existing and new assets and capabilities (largely ordinary), make them more rare, inimitable and not strategically substitutable and therefore increase their potential value contribution to a sustained organizational performance. Core capabilities are deployed when resources are oriented within the strategic orientation of the firm. Then in order to sustain the benefits achieved or respond to the threats (and/or opportunities) on core capabilities and performance of the firm, dynamic capabilities become necessary. These higher order capabilities therefore form part of a strategic process through which the firm develops, deploys and manages resources to sustain its performance in its rapidly changing or volatile business environment.

DYNAMIC CAPABILITIES FRAMEWORK

Though the resource-based theory is relevant in understanding resources, it is fairly quiet on how these resources are developed and deployed in firms. The notion that internal and external firm-specific resources, specifically capabilities, can be rebuilt or combined with other resources to develop new assets and capabilities lies in the dynamic capabilities framework, which until recent development by Teece at al. (1997) had been previously partially developed by Penrose (1959), Teece (1982) and Wernerfelt (1984).

The dynamic capabilities framework builds on theoretical foundations provided by Schumpeter (1934), Penrose (1959), Williamson (1975, 1985), Barney (1986), Nelson & Winter (1982) and Teece (1988) to give an understanding of how firms develop and renew their resources to be congruent to their rapidly changing environments (Dierickx & Cool, 1989; Prahalad & Hamel, 1990). Within this coherent framework, Teece *et al.* (1997: 518) argue that competitive advantage of a firm rests on its distinctive processes (managerial and organisational), and is shaped by its (specific) asset position, and the paths available to it by adoption or inheritance. The distinctive processes refer to the managerial and organisational processes by which things are done in the firm and in which the firm's capabilities are embedded; positions refer to the firm's current resource portfolio (owned and accessible); and paths refer to the strategic alternatives available to the firm. Capabilities and assets developed through paths should have the VRIN attributes to be considered as resources. Paths thus refer to the set of decision options through which capabilities and assets evolution occurs to create the significant outputs or the e-commerce benefits DC firms seek to achieve. This relates to our earlier conceptualisation of strategic orientation. Thus what a firm can do and where it can go tends to be constrained by its positions and paths (Teece *et al.*, 1997: 524). This tends to be congruent with our earlier argument that a firm's ability to create and sustain e-commerce benefits depends on both its resources and strategic orientation.

The understanding of how resources, specifically capabilities, evolve through a set of possible paths is theoretically characterised by the capability lifecycle (Helfat & Peteraf, 2003: 1000). The capability lifecycle is defined by three main stages consisting of: the founding, developing and maturity stage; and then, after the maturity stage, the capability can branch into one of at least six additional stages of the lifecycle; retirement (death), retrenchment, renewal, replication, redeployment, and recombination, which influence the future evolution of the capability.

At the ***founding stage,*** the organisation identifies the objective of creating a new resource or specifically a new capability. The organisation would primarily have to rely on existing resources, or its current processes (embedded capabilities) and positions to create the new resources. The new resource may be created through the combination of existing resources to generate new ones or acquisition of new resources which also depends on the access created by present resources such as financial and social capital. What is thus required of the firm at this stage is to identify the necessary current assets positions and processes and organise them around the objective of developing a new resource. These may include forming a team to develop the capability for the firm (Helfat & Peteraf, 2003: 1000).

In the ***developing stage,*** the firm is required to develop the resource through a search and examination of viable alternatives for resource development. Teece *et al.* (1997) explain from the dynamic capabilities framework that through coordination, learning and reconfiguration organisational processes or embedded capabilities are developed. *Coordination* stems from recognising and examining the congruencies and complementarities among existing resources or current processes, and between them and assets positions. By identifying distinct ways of combining or coordinating resources, firms can create unique or firm-specific resources which may be imperfectly mobile and rare among competing firms. Then again, *learning* through repetition and experimentation enables the firm to acquire the tacit knowledge to perform its processes better and quicker, for existing processes to be innovated and for new processes to be identified (Levitt & March, 1988). Learning occurs at the individual and collective or organisational levels and internally in the organisation and externally from trading partners and competing firms (Dixon, 2000). For all learning opportunities, mechanisms should be created to make knowledge accessible for application in the improvement of existing resources and development of new resources in the organisation. Lastly, *reconfiguration,* involves the examination of the rapidly changing environment of the firm to transform or reconfigure a firm's assets structure and processes to sustain their strategic value to the firm. This capacity of reconfiguring and transforming itself is a learned organisational skill which is gained through practice (Teece *et al.,* 1997). After this stage when the resource becomes a learned organisational skill, its development may cease and enter the maturity stage.

The ***maturity stage*** is concerned with the maintenance of the resource; a capability which involves a lot of exercising or usage of the capability for it to become more habitual, and embedded in organisational memory and culture. As the resource becomes more tacit in nature, the development may fade away in the organisation and conditions of causal ambiguity and social complexity are created around the resource, making it imperfectly mobile (Barney, 1991; Helfat & Peteraf, 2003). After the maturity stage, the resource branches into at least one of the six additional stages of the lifecycle due to threats to the resource or capability. *Retirement* occurs when threats or extreme conditions force the firm to retire the resource entirely like prohibition of the sale of a specific product may retire the resource – such as manufacturing plants – that were used in producing and delivering that product (Helfat and Peteraf, 2003: 1006). Where the threats are less severe and do not suddenly retire the resource, it may initiate a gradual reduced utilisation of the resource like falling demand for product, and thus lead to *retrenchment*. On the other hand, certain threats or crises can rather give the firm the motivation to seek to improve a resource through renewal, redeployment and recombination, instead of retiring it. Alternatively, the organisation might even seek to enter a new product or geographic market which may redevelop the retired or retrenched resource. *Renewal* of resource requires the firm to enter a new development stage and search, examine and develop new alternatives. Renewal may lead to modification of resource as new alternatives may define changes in processes and assets positions. *Redeployment* occurs when the resource is redeployed into a market for a different but closely related product. Such transfers would require an alteration of the resource to enable it serve a different product market. The resource would thus have to enter a new development stage for it to be redeployed.

The firm may also reproduce the same resource in a different geographic market, thus *replicating* the resource. Since barriers to replication exist, the firm may experience an initial drop in the level of the resource (capability), and then redevelop it back to its pre-replication level. *Recombination* occurs when original resources are combined with other resources to form new resources. This can occur during the renewal of resources in a current product market or in transferring the resource to a different but related market. Ideally, renewal, redeployment and recombination may lead to substantial alteration of the original resource and on further development create a new resource *relatively* distinct from the old one (Helfat & Peteraf, 2003: 1008).

In effect, the capability lifecycle lends the understanding to the paths through which resources are developed, deployed and managed to create and sustain significant outputs or e-commerce benefits. The ability of the firm to carry out these resource development processes depends on the higher order – core and dynamic – capabilities in the firm. Coordination and learning to develop resources may occur through the deployment of core capabilities, however, the reconfiguration of resources in response to changes in a firm's business environment and to sustain e-commerce benefits would occur through the deployment of dynamic capabilities.

Sample Studies Using RBT and DC

1. Boateng, R. (2016). Resources, Electronic-Commerce Capabilities and Electronic-Commerce Benefits: Conceptualizing the Links, *Information Technology for Development, 22*(6), 1-23.

2. Budu, J., and Boateng, R. (2015). Mobile Service Capabilities: evidence from a Ghanaian Mobile Service Provider. *International Journal of E-Services and Mobile Applications, 7*(3), 1-17.

3. Chakrabarty, S., & Wang, L. (2012). The long-term sustenance of sustainability practices in MNCs: A dynamic capabilities perspective of the role of R&D and internationalization. *Journal of business ethics, 110* (2), 205-217.

4. Chirico, F., & Nordqvist, M. (2010). Dynamic capabilities and trans-generational value creation in family firms: The role of organizational culture. *International Small Business Journal, 28*(5), 487-504.

5. Cui, L., Zhang, C., Zhang, C., & Huang, L. (2006). Exploring e-government impact on Shanghai firms' Informatisation Process, *Electronic Markets, 16*(4), 312-328.

6. Montealegre, R. (2002). A process model of capability development: Lessons from the electronic commerce strategy at Bolsa De Valores De Guayaquil. *Organization Science, 13*(5), 514-531.

7. Zhu, K. and Kraemer, K.L. (2005). Post-adoption variations in usage and value of e-business by organizations: Cross country evidence from the retail industry. *Information Systems Research, 16*(1), 61-84.

Research Gaps in RBT

To guide future RBT and Information Systems (IS) research, extant research have emphasised two gaps of concern to this research. First, whether IS resources (like IS infrastructure and technical skills which have gained much focus in IS literature), must interact with other constructs – non-IS resources (like firm reputation and brand) – to create e-commerce benefits (Wade & Hulland, 2004: 124). The emerging success stories noted above are also suggestive of other non-IS resources such as social-cultural capital and networks being key resources to e-commerce adoption. Hence, research exploring how such non-IS resources interact with IS resources to create e-commerce benefits will be a welcome contribution to knowledge. Second, there are blurred distinctions between resources that help firms *attain* and those that help firms *sustain* competitive advantage (or performance). Further empirical research is considered as being critical to provide an understanding of "how firms get to be good, how they sometimes stay that way, why and how they improve and why they sometimes decline" (Teece *et al.*, 1997: 530).

Research Gaps in DC

The theory has been criticized for a number of issues. First, it does not define properly the term 'dynamic capabilities' (Arend & Bromiley, 2009). Others such as Eisenhardt and Martin (2000) indicate that 'dynamic capabilities' has been used vaguely in the literature. Second, in explaining dynamic capabilities in the literature, the firm is portrayed as a good performing one. Some have argued that poor-performing firms can also have dynamic capabilities (Rindova & Kotha, 2001) but that do not lead to success. Also, change has been misconstrued as success, but in actual fact, just because a firm does not change, does not indicate that it lacks the dynamic capabilities to change (Arend & Bromiley, 2009). Third, the theory has also received considerable criticism for its problems with measuring dynamic capabilities (Williamson, 1999). Pavlou and El Sawy (2011) have emphatically noted that there is a lack of a measurement model for the theory.

Key Readings on RBT and DC

1. Barney, J. (1991). Firm resources and sustained competitive advantage. *Journal of Management, 17*(1), 99-120.

2. Teece, D. J., Pisano, G. and Shuen, A. (1997). Dynamic capabilities and strategic

management. *Strategic Management Journal, 18*(7), 509-533.

3. Wade, M. & Hulland, J. (2004). Review: The resource-based view and information systems research: Review, extension and suggestions for future research. *MIS Quarterly, 28*(1), 107-142.

4. Wang, C.L. & Ahmed, P.K. (2007). Dynamic capabilities: a review and research agenda, *International Journal of Management Reviews, 9*(1), 31-51.

Practice Question 18

1. Use the above theories to analyze the strategic behavior of managers in the case study outlined here – Kasadrin Company Limited.

Doing Business Online : Evidence From A Beverage Manufacturing Company

Kasadrin Company Limited - Firm Profile

Kasadrin Company Limited (KCL) was incorporated on March, 1987 after it had begun operations as a small-scale manufacturer of alcoholic and non-alcoholic beverages in 1986. The company focuses on producing alcoholic and non-alcoholic beverages to satisfy consumers, primarily in Ghana. KCL has 13 products. The company's indigenous products are Opeimu Bitters, Alomo Bitters, Alomo Root Wine, Kasadrin Dry Gin, Kasadrin Brandy, Kasadrin Tonic Wine, Kasapak, Cream Soda Mix, Lime Cordial, and Aperitif Sherry Red Wine. The other three products, Three Barrels Brandy, Pixie Dry Gin and Flavoured Cardinal Liqueurs, are produced by the company under license from a Dutch alcohol manufacturer. KCL's major products, or as termed 'flagship' products, are Alomo Bitters and Alomo Root Wine. Its indigenous products are developed through research-collaboration with the Centre for Scientific Research into Plant Medicine (CSRPM), Ghana.

The raw materials for the other products and other related materials for production are sourced both locally and internationally. Local sourcing is done by telephone and email and international or foreign sourcing is done electronically through the Internet and email, supported by telephone communication and frequent visits. Flavours are obtained from

France, metal and plastic caps from India, plastic laminates for pouch making/filling from India and glass bottles from Germany. Alcohol is supplied by another Ghanaian company which imports it from different countries including Brazil. The firm also uses the Internet to find information on how to maintain production machinery and source for spare parts from machine building companies in Germany.

Through an intra-organisational network system, the bottling and plant department is informed of the type and quantity of the product to be produced daily. The concentrates for the products are prepared and placed in the automated bottling processor. The respective bottles or sachets of the product are placed in the automated bottling processor consisting of four main stages; washing, filling, labelling and packaging. During these processes the products are regularly inspected by the quality assurance unit to identify bottles with low fills, bad capping/uncapped bottles, bottles with cracks from movement in the automated processor and bottles with twisted labels or wrong labels. Packaged products are placed into storage for distribution. After payments are made for product orders, the sales and marketing manager authorises goods to be delivered to distributors or individuals who are buying in large quantities, usually for an event. The firm distributes an average of 3,000,000 cartons of its products annually through a network of over 50 distributors.

KCL has three executive directors, who run the company with the support of seven managers who form the management team. The three executive directors consist of executive chairman, executive director and the managing director, who is also the founder of the company. The managing director (MD) is a graduate of EMPRETEC Ghana, an UNCTAD capacity-building programme for SMEs and entrepreneurial skills promotion. He is also an executive member of the Chartered Institute of Administration of Ghana. The executive chairman holds a PhD in agricultural economics and is a fellow of the Chartered Institute of Bankers (Ghana). The executive director has a bachelor's degree in electrical and electronic engineering and master's in business administration. KCL's executives are supported by a management team consisting of sales and marketing manager, bottling and plant manager, general manager for finance and accounting, purchasing and supply manager, marketing and public relations manager, general manager for operations, and information systems manager. These managers have postgraduate degrees and professional qualifications related to their respective managerial functions. The IT unit is made up of the IS manager and an IT technician. The IT unit is responsible for all IS-related issues. KCL has a permanent workforce of 101 who work in unison with approximately between 150 and 180 casual labourers yearly.

KCL has 30 workstations ranging from Pentium III to Pentium IV computers, connected to a network at the rate of 100Mbps. The firm obtained its first Internet subscription in 2001. It currently subscribes to a broadband Internet service from a local ISP – a speed of 512kps at a cost of US$120 a month. As a company policy, only the workstations of the executive, managers and secretaries have access to the Internet. KCL's email system is hosted by a local firm, CT Solutions, which also developed and hosts the company's website. For the procurement and management of the company's IT infrastructure and business systems, the company manages close working relationships with four trading partners, including CT Solutions.

KCL has been a member of the Ghana Club 100 since 2002. The Ghana Club 100 ranked the firm tenth in the manufacturing industry in 2003, and named the firm the second most profitable Ghanaian company in 2004, with a return on equity of 134 percent. In the overall rankings of the top 100 companies in Ghana, the firm placed sixteen in 2003; fifteen in 2004, and nine in 2005 (Ghana Club 100, 2004, 2005).

Business Start-Up

KCL began as a small-scale alcoholic beverage-manufacturing firm in the home of the MD in 1986. As at that time, alcoholic beverage production was dominated by foreign imports and products of two large Ghanaian manufacturers and about a hundred family-oriented small-scale (in-house) manufacturers located in Nungua, a suburb of Accra. Though, as compared to foreign imports, the quality of locally brewed alcohol by small-scale manufacturers was relatively lower, they received an appreciable patronage. Foreign imports were expensive and the production volume of the Ghanaian manufacturers could not satisfy the demand. As a result, there was a growing demand for good quality alcoholic drinks that were relatively affordable to the average Ghanaian. This market niche inspired the MD to start the company. According to the MD,

> 'This insight was unique; …we identified the increasing sophistication of the consumer. High expectations in terms of taste, quality, safety and packaging meant that the Ghanaian consumer was spending more on foreign imports that met their aspiration'.

The MD began the firm with three other close relations which included an ex-distillery worker who managed the production and two supporting staff for production and distribution. The MD was responsible for scouting customers, marketing, promoting and obtaining feedback from local drinking pubs. The number of employees became five when another friend joined the firm as the operations manager (also the current general manager for operations), managing daily operations of the firm, and doubling as the driver since he was the most knowledgeable about the capital city, Accra.

The first product was Kasadrin Gin. The name Kasadrin (pseudonym) was the appellation of a local chief in the Western region of Ghana (the MD's hometown). Kasadrin Gin became one of first locally named brands which were professionally packaged. Having an indigenous product which could match up to imported products was a potential sales and marketing factor for the company. KCL produced a total output of four cartons (64 litres) of Kasadrin gin per week. On his first day of doubling as a driver, the operations manager (OM) realised a caveat in the sales and marketing strategy. The company was selling and marketing its products during the normal working hours (8.00am to 5.00pm). However, within these times the owners of the bars and other public drinking places, who were primarily civil servants, were usually not available to make purchase decisions. This affected the sales of their products. Upon further discussions with the MD, it was decided that sales and marketing team change their working hours to the evening. The change gave the firm the opportunity to meet owners and part of the drinking community and introduce them to their products. The OM reflects that,

> 'The response was remarkable. Within one week, the company for its first time sold 20 cartons of Kasadrin Gin. For the owners of the public drinking places this was a welcome change in their operations; Kasadrin was serving them at their doorsteps, as compared to going to the established brewery companies and importers to purchase their products. As a new company with new brands of drinks this was the best option available to effectively market our products'.

Further, the local drinking pubs and alcoholic beverage retailers were also losing revenue from long waiting periods after making deposits to purchase imported products. Kasadrin therefore did not just offer a competing new brand, 'but became the readily available drink' (Interview with Nungua Local Resident (since 1987), AX Enterprise, 18 November, 2006). After a year, the company bought another van for sales, marketing and distribution. The MD and OM recruited new staff and trained them to manage the sales, marketing and distribution. On appointment, the new sales and marketing manager made another observation concerning the public advertisement of alcoholic products. The sales and marketing manager comments that,

> '…because of tax evasion some Ghanaian firms stayed away from public adverts, however, Kasadrin saw this as an opportunity and actively engaged in the public advertisement of their

products. This increased the patronage of our products'.

As a registered company which adhered to tax responsibilities, KCL began to publicly advertise its products through the local media. This gave KCL some competitive edge over the other small-scale manufacturers which avoided such marketing opportunities. A tax officer at the Ghana VAT office confirmed that as part of the strategies for curbing tax evasion, the local media is monitored consistently to identify firms who are not listed in their databases. She notes that, 'It is very common to find many small businesses avoiding public advertisement in the local media because of tax issues. These firms also avoid trade exhibitions. Though these are opportunities of expanding their market reach, they do not want their activities to be monitored by tax agencies or officials in Ghana' (Interview with Tax Officer, Ghana VAT Office, 4 December 2006). Additionally, the MD also introduced sales commissions and awards for meeting targets, which increased the commitment of the sales and marketing team, encouraging them to sell more of the products. The employees received commission on meeting sales targets and an extra commission for each sale beyond the sales target.

In the 1990's KCL focused on two major projects;

- Collaborating with CSPRM to explore the development of products from alcoholic extracts from traditional plants. Two products, Alomo Bitters and Alomo Root Wine, were introduced in 1999. The Alomo Bitters brand was awarded the Chartered Institute of Marketing, Ghana (CIMG) Product of the Year 1999 Award. The success of the collaboration between KCL and CSRPM also led to the research and development of Opeimu Bitters in 2005.

- Building an automated production factory with an administrative office block. The firm moved into the new factory premises in 2000 and the building was commissioned in 2001.

Thereafter, KCL changed its strategy from production, distribution and marketing to focus on their core objective of producing alcoholic and non-alcoholic beverages in 2003. Two issues necessitated the change in strategy. First, there was growing competition from foreign liquor and local manufacturers. A number of companies, including the local subsidiary of an international brewery company, had developed substitute products with indigenous Ghanaian names. Hence, the product and marketing strategy of KCL had been partly imitated. Second, the sales and marketing activities needed to go beyond Accra and the Southern sector of Ghana to the Northern sector. The Northern sector contributed only about one percent of the company's total sales. As a result, the firm changed its strategy to focus on production while supporting the distributors, who did the sales of products, with marketing and promotion.

The competitive strategy of KCL's competitors connotes with the Resource Based Theory's argument of creating substitute products to compete with that of the seeming successful firm. In this case, competing firms understood that creating socio-cultural connotation and relationships around their products was necessary to compete with the products of KCL. The general manager for finance and accounting (GFA) explains that, though KCL's net profit after tax increased by 42 percent in 2005, competition from foreign liquor and local producers made the industry very competitive leading to the decline in turn-over by 31 percent as compared to that of 2004.

Exploring Export Opportunities

In 2004, the firm began to receive distributorship and purchase enquiries via email and telephone from potential customers from other countries in West Africa, Europe and the USA. These enquiries were usually from Ghanaians who operated African or Ghanaian shops, drinking avenues and restaurants. The products usually requested for exports were Alomo Bitters and Opeimu Bitters. However, as of that time, the firm had no official organisational strategy to export outside the country. Products had usually been purchased and exported by Ghanaians living abroad and other foreigners at their own cost and usually for personal use. This was usually in small quantities and done with distributors, without the collaboration of the firm. Contributory reasons for the lack of an organisational export strategy were the untapped opportunities in Northern Ghana and the existence of a number of process issues within export trade. These process issues refer to meeting export-trade requirements and expectations of the export market while keeping the originality of the product. The sales and marketing manager comments that,

> 'The Internet has done its work in broadening the market, however there are key issues related to the import of alcoholic beverages which differs across the various countries. For example, the European Union had certain standards for importing alcoholic beverages especially in relation to alcohol levels. These products and related trading requirements are partly the issues stalling the exports of our brands'.

The failure to meet diverse export and product standards of developed countries has been argued as one of the major challenges of developing country (DC) firms, and may therefore affect their ability to increase their market reach through the Internet (Todaro and Smith, 2003: 575; Molla *et al.*, 2006b). Though the Internet had aided in initiating export trade enquiries through information on the firm's website and email communication, it was not enough to facilitate the export process. In 2005, KCL shipped two forty-foot containers, approximately 5000 cartons of Alomo Bitters to the USA after meeting a number of export trade requirements. This was a result of an email request by an interested customer to be sold in African shops and drinking places. In order to facilitate this order, the customer was referred to a US firm which was partly owned by the managing director of KCL. The US firm became the liaison between the customer and KCL; enabling KCL to acquire the necessary certification and facilitating pre- and post-contractual agreements. In the marketing manager's assessment,

> 'The customer was relatively determined to work with KCL through all the procedural stages in meeting all requirements and obtaining all the licenses required to export the products. The process is usually detailed and could take a number of months; some potential customers become disinterested as it becomes more costly in terms of time and resources'.

Extant literature shows that the lack of commitment, trust and compliance mechanisms affects decision-making and contributes to the loss of contracts and contractual disputes in transactions in the marketplace (Pare, 2003). Hence, the provision of the requisite measures to motivate actors participating in online transactions becomes critical. After realising the potential of the US market, KCL commissioned sales agents with sample products to study the foreign markets, specifically USA, Europe and West Africa in 2006. A primary issue indicated by the studies in the USA and Europe relates to the differences in product packaging across countries/regions. For example, in the USA market, customers found the long and big bottles of Alomo Bitters uncomfortable, since they were more accustomed to buying from the shelves and drinking from the bottle. The customers preferred the smaller bottles which they could easily carry and take sips from. In the European Union market, there was a preference for PET (Polyethylene Terephthalate) bottles, which are very lightweight, and more technically and practically recyclable as compared to glass bottles.

In West Africa, KCL identified a potential market for its products in countries which have had their nationals living in Ghana for a period by virtue of war and trade. Some of these nationals had experienced their products and were back in their countries. KCL decided to focus on recruiting distributors in these countries. KCL commissioned two sales representatives, one to work in francophone countries; Ivory Coast and Togo, and the other to work in Nigeria, Liberia, and Sierra Leone. The credibility of a prospective distributor was to be established through letters of credit through KCL's bankers and information from the trade missions of the countries involved. As of July 2007, two prospective distributors from Liberia and Nigeria had visited KCL to ascertain its production capacity in meeting their requirements before making a substantial investment in exports and distribution. These business considerations are yet to turn into transactions of financial value. Communication between the firm and the sales representatives has been supported by emails and telephone.

E-commerce Capabilities Development

The development of e-commerce capabilities in KCL can be traced in two main stages of developing informational and interactional e-commerce capabilities.

Informational E-commerce Capability (Jan 2001 – Dec 2001)

The firm considered building an informational e-commerce capability after adopting a connected form of e-commerce. The MD and the other firm managers had begun to use the Internet as a medium for sourcing production materials and equipment suppliers. Email was used to initiate business relationships with these suppliers and support transactions and negotiations with other trading partners in Europe and India. The firm had no IT manager. Internet access was being obtained from local cybercafés and this was not convenient, timely or efficient for the firm's productivity. The objective of the firm at this stage was to connect to the Internet and to create an online presence. The MD signed up for a dial-up package with a local ISP. The operations manager reflects that,

> 'At that time we only had two PCs, one used by the MD and another, shared by the rest of the managers. Only the MD's computer was connected to the Internet. To send an email you had to go to the MD's office and when you receive your emails, you either download them onto diskette or print them out directly'.

It was during this regular use of the Internet that they considered the Internet as a potential channel relevant for marketing and promotional activities. As most of the firm's foreign suppliers and trading partners had a website or online presence in related industry directories, creating an online presence through a website and other online directories became a pertinent objective for the company. Additionally, Alomo Bitters, the firm's major product, had been named the 1999 product of the year by CIMG. The firm therefore considered marketing its brands and itself globally through the Internet. Consequently, the firm contracted its ISP to design a website for the firm. The website consisted of three main web pages: a) Home/About Us – description of company with its activities; b)

Products – product description; and c) Contact Us – company's contact details. The expected value was the firm's perceived benefits of an online presence and visibility. The website was hosted by the ISP, as a sub-domain under the ISP's domain – http://www.aoghana.com.gh/kasadrin. An email address was created for the firm based on the ISP's domain. The website was allocated 10mb server space and email address – kasadrin@aoghana.com.gh. Its usage statistics were not monitored and no updates were done on the website in 2001.

In summary, we identify three key actions used by the firm to acquire resources and use them to develop an informational e-commerce capability which further supported or partly enabled the achievement of informational and operational benefits. The actions are:

- Learning from trading partners;

- Using external IS resources to address internal IS resource poverty; and

- Using Internet and email to support core activities such as sourcing and maintaining business relationships with production material suppliers.

The informational and operational benefits partly enabled by the capability are creating an online presence and marketing the firm's products; and initiating and supporting transactions and business relationships with production material suppliers.

Interactional E-commerce Capability (Jan 2002 – Jul 2007)

The development of an interactional e-commerce capability in KCL is characterised by two interrelated stages: development of an IS infrastructure which facilitated the implementation of an IT strategy which included developing an interactive website. First, KCL sought to automate its internal operations and business processes. The firm purchased a bundle of software – accounting, payroll, and a fleet management system from a local IT software development firm, PERF. PERF was responsible for upgrading KCL's existing IT infrastructure – buying computers and networking them to support the running of the software. When the project was completed the firm realised they needed an IT support staff or team to manage the IS infrastructure. KCL asked the project manager to develop an IT strategy for the firm and later recruited the project manager as their IS manager. Another IT technician was also recruited to work in unison with the IS manager. These human and technical resources became a precursory foundation to enable the firm to enhance its IT capabilities and develop other e-commerce capabilities including the design of an interactive website.

On appointment, the IS manager (hereafter referred to as Sarah) began to implement the IT strategy which included subscription to a broadband Internet service (2003), the development of an interactive website (2003), and initiation of an enterprise resource planning system to integrate all data and functional processes in the firm (2006-2008). In developing the website, Sarah researched websites of beverage companies (worldwide) in order to get ideas to inform the content. Sarah comments that,

> 'The old website was very basic and compared to the websites of other foreign beverage companies, it was less informative and had spelling mistakes. It was not a good representation of the company's growing reputation, locally and internationally'.

After the research, the design concepts were discussed with CT Solutions, whom the project was outsourced to. A proposal with a preliminary design developed through this collaboration was presented to the firm's management team for an evaluation. The website was considered as a critical part of the company's measures to respond to the growing competition in the industry. Decisions made on the website included the choice of colour, the graphics and the content; the choice of a Flash-based website for fast Internet connection and a non-Flash-based website for slow Internet connection; and the integration of the firm's local distributorship network into the website content (in the form of an online directory). In reference to the company's commitment to social responsibility, a caution on being of a legal drinking age before entering the site was incorporated in the website design. The new website was designed by June 2003. A new domain name was registered – www.kasadringh.com. It was hosted on a 1000MB server web space in the USA through CT Solutions. The company pays US$60 a month for the web hosting. The website consisted of six main web pages:

- Products Page – detailed description of all products;

- Company Page – provides information on the company mission, vision and board of directors;

- Distributors Page – a directory listing the contact details of distributors by region and offering downloadable application forms;

- News – latest news and events on the company's products and activities;

- Downloads – offers wallpapers on company products;

- Contact Us – offers an enquiry form to make enquiries and provides contact information and location direction to the firm.

Exhibit 31 Homepage of the www.kasadringh.com (flash version).

Though there was no search functionality on the website, a product combo-box was placed on the homepage to facilitate easy navigation to any product. In addition to the main pages of the website, there are three other sub-pages; Media Room, Events and Cocktails. These pages were used to create a form of social connotation or interaction with the firm's potential customers/consumers of their products. Media room made available video adverts run through TV networks, and the cocktails page featured related cocktails which could be prepared with their products. Information on all offline events and promotions of products are also made available online on the Events Page. The firm also attempted to increase its visibility by providing a view of its production process and information on quality assurance procedures employed by the firm. However, this seems to have relatively had a minimal impact, since it is only a slideshow of three pictures depicting the production process. When questioned on using a better presentation medium, such as video, the Plant and Bottling manager explains that,

> 'We are, perhaps, the first or one of the first alcoholic beverage manufacturers in Ghana to develop a complete wall-to-wall automation of its production line, from bottling to packaging. Hence, for competitive reasons, the firm has reservations of making a public display of its machines in its production line. We therefore considered a few pictures of certain sections of the production line were enough to show our production line'.

Porter (1985: 33-34) states that: '...A firm gains competitive advantage by performing these strategically important activities more cheaply or better than its competitors'. Hence, in view of other competing products, the seeming objective was to protect knowledge on core resources and other key organisational information which help create this advantage from competitors. Thus, combining the automated production line with other organisational resources like research and development of new products (as done with Opeimu Bitters in 2005), and marketing (as done with the indigenous naming system for products) and managerial skills and knowledge, the firm can create a capability, such as market responsiveness (in product line), which may be rare across the competitors in the market (Santhanam and Hartono, 2003).

This reservation or relative sensitivity to the kind (and detail) of information made available on the Internet was also extended to information on KCL's financial performance, production volume and sales information. Notwithstanding, the OM argues that,

> The reservations placed on publishing information on organisational performance and production capacity was relevant in designing the website as of 2003, however much has changed since then. Other leading manufacturing firms in Ghana are making available their press releases of performance both in local press and on their websites. By providing this information, we have a better chance of enhancing the reputation and credibility we seek to create online and inform the decision-making process of prospective trading partners and customers'.

Incomplete or asymmetrical information could affect decision-making related to purchase which may lead to loss of contracts and contractual disputes (Pare, 2003). Hence, providing inadequate information affects the capability of using informational resources like the company's website to enhance the decision making of prospective customers and trading partners.

The challenge in using the website is to do with its management. The average number of page views per month was 148 in 2004; 227 (2005) and 348 (2006). Between 2003 and 2006, there have only been three major updates. The updates were done when a department – Human Resources, IT or Marketing – of the company needed to post new content on the website such as events and news. When questioned on the management of the website, Sarah comments that,

> 'I face a difficult situation of trying to convince the management on allocating more human resources for IT. I have requested for additional staff the past three years and this has not been met. From my observation, management responds to IT initiatives if only it is a recommendation by an external IT expert or consultant. For example, a request to buy and use corporate licensed copies of Microsoft products instead of single licensed or pirated copies installed by hired IT technicians were ignored until the Microsoft official representative in Ghana sent in a letter concerning a software inspection exercise. Hence, I have had to use consultants to initiate IT projects, such as upgrading software and purchasing new infrastructure. Concerning the website, CT Solutions does not have enough interaction with us, as a client. After the website was designed, there was no further relationship and we were not advised on the management of the website. CT Solutions only contacts us when there is a need to renew the web hosting contract or any other form of service which requires payment. Moreover, we receive about 10 emails each week on new enquiries concerning our products and business activities, but since there is no specific employee to respond and follow-up on these enquiries, we just forward them to the head of department of relevance. This often leads to information overload and some of the enquiries are therefore not attended to. The IT unit does not have resources to monitor the state of the enquiry and similar or related enquiries are made over time repetitively. If analysed the website could have been updated with the relevant information to relatively reduce the enquiries or make enquiries more relevant. As a result, we (the IT unit), do what we can with the limited resources'.

Previous literature has noted that scarcity of skilled personnel or the requisite IS human resources tends to be a limiting factor to the development and management of e-business within firms in developing countries (Singh and Gilchrist, 2002). To address the internal resource poverty, these firms use IT consultancies to create this online presence. However, IT consultancies, who are usually responsible for designing and hosting the websites, fail to give these firms any reports on website traffic and strategic advice on Internet marketing after the websites are developed. This could affect the achievement of expected value and the continuity of projects. The manager of CT Solutions argues that,

> 'There was no specific contract concerning the management of the website, hence there was no agreed deliverables. The firm paid US$60 monthly for the web hosting. The fact is that firms have poor understanding of the Internet. Most companies seek projects that deliver

immediate results. Websites in this part of the world are not transactional, they are mostly used for branding, image promotion and information provision. We don't have the supporting systems for transactional websites. Hence, the firms do not put much value on websites since the results are not apparently immediate. Additionally, most organisations do not have a coherent web strategy that we can inform.

What we, website developer firms, do, is to translate the website strategy of the firm into reality. With our experience, we can relatively suggest or recommend to companies about what they can do. Therefore, we provide some level of consultancy, but since the Internet is not tangible and we do not have privy access to all business information and processes, it is difficult to quantify returns to the firm. Moreover, most Ghanaian firms do not consider the Internet as their core business. Hence, because of this lack of intimacy, the switching costs are low and many firms do change their IT solution partners as soon as they fail to deliver or get disappointed about their services. That is the major challenge the firms face, the market (IT sector) is different here in Ghana'.

We note from the above that the social reputation, credibility and image of KCL tend to influence the choice of e-commerce technologies and allocation of resources to facilitate adoption and use. Thus, perhaps, without an apparent threat to these social resources, resource allocation for an e-commerce project may be stalled or considered less necessary. Faced with such constraints, the negotiation skills of KCL's IS manager became necessary to ensure the continuity of projects. For example, in January 2007, this impasse between KCL and CT Solutions was resolved after a management meeting was arranged internally between the IT Unit and management team and externally between the KCL and CT Solutions. The IS manager argued on the necessity to update the website in time for Ghana's Independence anniversary (in which KCL was a key sponsor). The OM also emphasised the need to advertise the new fluorescent bottle cap for Opeimu Bitters, which had been changed in response to the piracy of the product. As part of this update, the flash website was dropped, and a non-flash website was updated with new pictures and navigation buttons to every part of the website. The flash website was dropped because, as compared to the non-flash website, it required more time and detail to be updated and the firm did not have the internal requisite skill and time availability to perform such updates. Dropping the flash website was therefore a response to the resource poverty in the firm. The firm was also provided with a simple administrative interface for updates and editing of content.

In summary, we identify five key actions used by the firm to acquire resources and use them to develop an interactional e-commerce capability which further enabled the achievement of largely strategic and informational benefits. The actions are:

1. Investing in requisite IT infrastructure;

2. Enhancing managerial business and IS knowledge and skills with new employees;

3. Prototyping website with knowledge from global benchmarks in the beverage industry;

4. Integrating the local distributorship network into website content; and

5. Joint evaluation of website (interactive) content by management and the IS consultant.

The informational and operational benefits partly enabled by the capability are creating an online presence and marketing the firm's products; and initiating and supporting transactions and business relationships with production material suppliers. Further, these benefits generated strategic benefits in terms of:

- Export of 5000 cartons of Alomo Bitters generated through an email request;

The other strategic benefits are:

- New product development and cost-savings from curbing product piracy through a partnership (email initiated and sustained) with an Indian bottle cap manufacturer; and

- Supporting firm policy of having two key suppliers for production materials through sourcing and maintaining relationships with production material suppliers.

What benefits is the company obtaining from e-commerce adoption?

....

....

....

....

....

....

....

....

....

....

....

....

....

....

....

....

....

....

What strategic decisions led to the adoption and usage e-commerce in the company?

....

....

....

....

....

....

....

....

....

....

....

....

....

....

....

....

....

....

....

....

....

....

....

....

Do you consider the existence of dynamic capabilities in the company? Explain your answer?

....

....

....

....

....

....

....

....

....

....

....

....

....

....

....

....

....

What IS policies will recommend for the company in order to sustain the benefits of e-commerce and advance beyond the current phase of adoption?

....

....

....

....

....

....

....

....

CHAPTER SUMMARY

The chapter explored discussed two theories used in analyzing the strategic behavior or decisions of firms. These theories - Resource-Based Theory (RBT) and Dynamic Capabilities (DC) Framework - have received much attention in strategic management and business studies, and are relevant in examining the strategic behavior of firms. RBT tends to be the prevailing paradigm that explains or helps to understand how and why firms develop the capability to gain and sustain competitive advantage. Its later extension, the dynamic capabilities approach examines how these firms adapt and even capitalize on rapidly changing technological or volatile environments as in DCs. Within the two theories, rival firms are viewed to compete on the basis of their internal characteristics, resources, through which they build competitive advantage and a superior long-term performance. By use of the case of a Ghanaian beverage manufacturing company, we have explored the strategic decisions and behavior of managers in the identification of opportunity, and development of resources to align IT/IS to business objectives, there improving their competitiveness in the marketplace.

Model Examination Questions

QUESTION 1

In reference to the Corporate Executive in Residence Seminar held in the second semester of the 2015/2016 academic year, it was argued that, technology is not so important in the deployment and management of information systems. Using relevant examples, explain your view on this argument.

QUESTION 2

You have been approached by University of Ghana to develop a social media policy to govern the responsible and strategic usage of social media applications by the university's website development and management team. Discuss the relevance of the following components of the social media policy:

a) Authorisation and Scope

b) Rationale

c) Principles

d) Stakeholder Involvement

QUESTION 3

Using relevant examples, develop a Bring Your Own Device (BYOD) to work policy for the usage of smartphones in the workplace.

QUESTION 4

Formal information system strategies are often absent or scarce in micro and small organizations. Discuss two reasons for this scarcity and outline the measures to address them.

QUESTION 5

Using relevant examples, discuss the interrelationships between business strategy, information systems strategy, and information systems alignment.

QUESTION 6

Managing Student Records in Kwaebibirem University

Over the past few years the examination office of the Kwaebibirem University has had a problem of making certificates to students on demand. Usually 80% of the graduating class requests their provisional certificates before the graduation ceremony. This often resulted in long periods of waiting and worst of all, faulty certificates. The examination office is responsible for issuing student certificates and therefore the office keeps records of students and their graduation details. To obtain this information, the office requests for information on final year students from the faculties. This includes the name, programme of study, year of admission. These are prepared by faculty examination officers and delivered in printed reports. On receiving this information, secretaries in the examination office make an electronic record file in Microsoft Word, by typing in all the information.

At the end of the academic year, the faculty examination officers submit results of the students to the University Academic Board. Approved results are then forwarded to the examination office. From the approved results, the final grades of students are obtained. The secretaries match the final grade with the records of students in the record file and print out a copy for each member of the staff of the examination office. The Chief Examination Officer (CEO) and his deputy, then do a thorough check of the records. After all identified errors are reconciled, printed copy of the records are filed. In order to obtain their provisional certificates, students apply to the examination office and collect them the next day. The secretaries match out the name on the application with the printed record file and they prepare the provisional certificate. The examination office sends the same record file to the University Public Relations office, which uses the file to publish the graduation handbook. They also send a list of final year students generated from the record list to the National Service Secretariat. The same record file is used to produce the final certificates issued during the graduation ceremony. Frequently, the Vice-Chancellor's office (VCO) requests for information from the examination office. The VCO has diverse needs, from data for simple to complex statistical analysis to produce official reports and sometimes support political views, motivations and interests.

It is estimated that the examination office receives 20 requests for provisional certificates per day. Out of this only 17 (85%) correct certificates are delivered the next day. The other 3 (15%) are either not delivered or even if they are, tend to be faulty. Usually students complain of errors in the provisional certificates which also reflect in the graduation handbook and to the final certificates if not corrected. The errors are often omitted names, mismatching grades and spelling mistakes. From the 15% not delivered, it is estimated that 13.5% is due to errors generated within the examination office and the remaining 1.5% is from the faculties.

On the other hand, the Vice-Chancellor has begun an administrative redesign throughout the whole University; as such the CEO is under much pressure to improve the efficiency of his office in order to keep his job. The secretaries are quite dissatisfied on having to type information on over 2000 students twice each academic year, notwithstanding the critical role these information plays in other functions of the University.

Question 6A

Using the above preamble, develop an IS Policy and a Strategic IS Plan for Kwaebibriem University to address the management of students records. Use the framework for the development of IS Policy and Strategic IS plan discussed the semester.

Question 6B

In reference to the above case study, outline three (3) challenges in implementing the IS policy and strategy you developed or proposed for Kwaebibirem University.

Question 6C

In reference to the above case study, outline (3) controls for information classification and handling in relation to the management of students' records.

QUESTION 7

It is argued that strategic information systems planning is complex, there is not a single best approach, and arriving at a single best approach for a specific organization is nearly impossible. As a result, many organizations utilize a combination of approaches or try to find the best fit approach for a given IT strategy. Using relevant examples, explain your view on this argument.

QUESTION 8

The Government of Ghana seeks to develop a national indentification platform which combines existing indentification systems of the National Indentification Authority, National Health Insurace Indentification Card and Voter's Indentification Card. Discuss three (3) implications of this initiative to national information technology policies.

QUESTION 9

As an IT consultant, outline and discuss the key components of an Internet Usage policy relevant to the use of the Internet and its related technologies by a Ghanaian University. Your answer should cover a minimum of three internet related applications such as website, social media and email.

QUESTION 10

You have been given GHS 30,000 to implement the strategic plan for an information systems policy and strategy that you developed for your firm. Assuming your company is a microfinance company, develop a budget for the rollout of the strategic plan. Provide brief notes to explain the purpose of each budget line.

QUESTION 11

Develop an e-mail and social media policy for the Office of the President of Ghana.

QUESTION 12

Formal information system strategies are often absent or scarce in micro and small organizations. Discuss two reasons for this scarcity and outline the measures to address them.

Works Cited

[1]   MindfulSecurity, "What are Policies, Standards, Guidelines and Procedures?," 02 04 2009. [Online]. Available: http://mindfulsecurity.com/2009/02/03/policies-standards-and-guidelines/.

[2]   K. Laudon and J. Laudon, Management Information Systems: Managing the Digital Firm. 11th Edition, Upper Saddle River, NJ 07458: Pearson Education Inc., 2010.

[3]   Western Michigan University;, "Information Technology Rules and Policies," Office of Information Technology, [Online]. Available: https://wmich.edu/it/policies. [Accessed 14 01 2017].

[4]   University of Chichester, "Support and Information Zone, University of Chichester," University of Chichester, [Online]. Available: http://help.chi.ac.uk/strategy-and-policies. [Accessed 14 01 2017].

[5]   M. Gregg, CISA Exam Prep: Certified Information Systems Auditor, Pearson IT Certification, 2007.

[6]   Amazon, "About Our Returns Policies," Amazon.com, 2017. [Online]. Available: https://www.amazon.com/gp/help/customer/display.html?nodeId=15015721. [Accessed 14 01 2017].

[7]   University of California, "Policies, Information Technology Services," 2017. [Online]. Available: http://www.ucop.edu/information-technology-services/policies/index.html. [Accessed 14 01 2017].

[8]   Highland Bank, "Homepage," [Online]. Available: https://www.highlandbanks.com/. [Accessed 14 01 2017].

[9]   ITManagerDaily, "Password Policy Template," 6 11 2013. [Online]. Available: http://www.itmanagerdaily.com/password-policy-template/. [Accessed 13 01 2017].

[10] D. Chaffey, "Global social media research summary 2016," 20 12 2016. [Online]. Available: http://www.smartinsights.com/social-media-marketing/social-media-strategy/new-global-social-media-research/. [Accessed 01 02 2017].

[11] M. Henricks, "Why You Need a Social Media Policy, Marketing Boot Camp, Entrepreneur," 06 01 2011. [Online]. Available: https://www.entrepreneur.com/article/217813. [Accessed 01 02 2017].

[12] P. D. Godec, "Ten Little-Known Concerns for Employers About Social Media," 08 06 2012. [Online]. Available: http://www.avvo.com/legal-guides/ugc/ten-little-known-concerns-for-employers-about-social-media. [Accessed 21 02 2014].

[13] adidas Group, "adidas Group Social Media Guidelines," [Online]. Available: http://blog.adidas-group.com/wp-content/uploads/2011/06/adidas-Group-Social-Media-Guidelines1.pdf. [Accessed 22 01 2017].

[14] Reuters, "Reuters' Reporting from the Internet and Using Social Media," 16 06 2016. [Online]. Available: http://handbook.reuters.com/index.php?title=Reporting_From_the_Internet_And_Using_Social_Media.

[Accessed 01 02 2017].

[15] Highland Bank, "ID Theft," 2016. [Online]. Available: https://www.highlandbanks.com/idtheft. [Accessed 14 01 2017].

[16] Highland Bank, "Technical Requirements," 2016. [Online]. Available: https://www.highlandbanks.com/technicalrequirements. [Accessed 14 01 2017].

[17] Standard Chartered, "Standard Chartered Group Code of Conduct," [Online]. Available: https://www.sc.com/en/resources/global-en/pdf/sustainabilty/Code_of_Conduct.pdf. [Accessed 14 01 2017].

[18] M. Berry, "BYOD Policy Template," [Online]. Available: http://www.itmanagerdaily.com/byod-policy-template/. [Accessed 1 02 2017].

[19] CIO, "Acceptable Use Policy Template," [Online]. Available: http://www.cio.ca.gov/OIS/Government/Library/documents/ACCEPTABLEUSEPOLICYTEMPLATE.doc. [Accessed 12 01 2017].

[20] Brown University, "Network Connection Policy," 01 2017. [Online]. Available: https://it.brown.edu/computing-policies/network-connection-policy. [Accessed 01 02 2017].

[21] The Institute of Education Sciences, "Web Publishing Guidelines, Forum Unified Education Technology Institute," [Online]. Available: https://nces.ed.gov/pubs2005/tech_suite/app_C.asp. [Accessed 22 01 2017].

[22] The Institute of Education Sciences, "Appendix D: Sample Security Agreements," [Online]. Available: https://nces.ed.gov/pubs2005/tech_suite/app_D.asp. [Accessed 01 02 2017].

[23] SANS Security Policy Resource Page, "SANS Security Policy Templates," 17 08 2016. [Online]. Available: https://www.sans.org/security-resources/policies. [Accessed 01 02 2017].

[24] R. Stim, "What is Fair Use? culled from the book Getting Permission (October 2010) by Richard Stim," 2010. [Online]. Available: http://fairuse.stanford.edu/overview/fair-use/what-is-fair-use/. [Accessed 01 02 2017].

[25] DP Policy, "Data Protection Template, Department of Education & Skills," [Online]. Available: https://www.education.ie/en/Schools-Colleges/Information/Post-Primary-School-Policies/data_protection_template.doc. [Accessed 01 02 2017].

[26] University of Michigan, " IT Policy Development and Administration Framework," 16 12 2016. [Online]. Available: http://cio.umich.edu/policy/policy-development-framework.

[27] L. Applegate, R. Austin and D. Soule, Corporate Information Strategy and Management, 8th ed., Burr Ridge, IL: McGraw-Hill/Irwin, 2009.

[28] C. Pitelis and A. Pseiridis, "Transaction Costs Versus Resource Value?," *Journal of Economic Studies,* vol. 26, no. 3, pp. 221-240, 1999.

[29] E. Park, "What Health Care Can Learn From Amazon," 16 02 2014. [Online]. Available:

http://www.recode.net/2014/2/26/11623948/what-health-care-can-learn-from-amazon. [Accessed 01 02 2017].

[30] Datafloq, "How Amazon Is Leveraging Big Data," 24 01 2017. [Online]. Available: https://datafloq.com/read/amazon-leveraging-big-data/517. [Accessed 31 01 2017].

[31] R. Boateng, R. Heeks, A. Molla and R. Hinson, "E-commerce and Socio-Economic Development: Conceptualizing the Link," *Internet Research,* vol. 18, no. 5, p. 562–592, 2008.

[32] M. Rundale, "Nike LunarGlide+ 5 iD Review: What It's Really Like To Make Your Own Running Shoes," [Online]. Available: www.huffingtonpost.co.uk/2013/07/24/nike-id-review-lunarglide_n_3643907.html. [Accessed 23 09 2013].

[33] NIKEiD, "NIKEiD," [Online]. Available: https://en.wikipedia.org/wiki/NikeID. [Accessed 01 02 2017].

[34] J. Bryson, Strategic Planning for Public and Nonprofit Organizations: A Guide to Strengthening and Sustaining Organizational Achievement, vol. 1, San Francisco, CA: Jossey-Bass, 2011.

[35] M. J. Earl, Management Strategies for Information Technology,, London: Prentice Hall, 1989.

[36] M. Klouwenberg, W. Koo and J. van Schaik, "Establishing business strategy with information technology," *Information Management & Computer Security,* vol. 3, no. 5, pp. 8-10, 1995.

[37] A. L. Lederer and V. Sethi, "Meeting the challenges of information systems planning," *Long Range Planning,* vol. 25, no. 2, pp. 60-80, 25.

[38] W. R. King, Planning for Information Systems, Advances in Management Information Systems, New York: M.E, Sharpe, Inc., 2009.

[39] F. Al-boud, "Strategic Information Systems Planning : A Brief Review," *International Journal of Computer Science and Network Security,* vol. 11, no. 5, pp. 179-183, 2011.

[40] H. E. Newkirk, A. L. Lederer and C. Srinivasan, "Strategic Information Systems Planning: too little or too much," *Journal of Strategic Information Systems,* vol. 12, pp. 201-228, 2003.

[41] G. Mentzas, "Implementing an IS strategy—a team approach," *Long Range Planning,* vol. 10, no. 1, p. 84–95, 1997.

[42] R. Rainer, C. Cegielski and B. Prince, Introduction to Information Systems: Supporting and Transforming Business, 3rd edition Canada Edition, Canada: John Wiley and Sons Inc., 2010.

[43] J. Ward and J. Peppard, Strategic Planning for Information Systems, 3rd Edition, New York: Wiley, 2002.

[44] R. Galliers, "Strategic Information Systems Planning: myths, reality and guidelines for successful implementation," *European Journal of Information Systems,* vol. 1, no. 1, pp. 55-64, 1991.

[45] R. Nolan and F. McFarlan, "Information Technology and the Board of Directors," *Harvard Business Review,* vol. 83, no. 10, pp. 96-106, 2005.

[46] F. McFarlan and J. McKenny, Corporate Information Management: The issues facing senior management, US: Irwin, 1983.

[47] N. Venkatraman and V. Ramanujam, "Planning system success: a conceptualization and an operational model," *Management Science,* vol. 33, no. 6, p. 687–705, 1987.

[48] A. Segars and V. Grover, "Strategic information systems planning success: an investigation of the construct and its measurements," *MIS Quarterly,* vol. June, p. 139–163, 1998.

[49] Amazon Web Services, "Unilever Case Study - Amazon Case Studies," [Online]. Available: https://aws.amazon.com/solutions/case-studies/. [Accessed 12 02 2017].

[50] J. Henderson and N. Venkatraman, "Strategic Alignment: Leveraging Information Technology for Transforming Organizations," *IBM Systems Journal,* 1999.

[51] J. Luftman, "Assessing Business-IT Alignment Maturity," *Communications of AIS,* vol. 4, no. 14, 2000.

[52] Comindwork, "Henderson and Venkatraman Strategic IT-Business Alignment Model," 5 12 2016. [Online]. Available: http://www.comindwork.com/weekly/2016-12-05/productivity/strategic-it-alignment. [Accessed 03 02 2017].

[53] J. Luftman, R. Papp and T. Brier, "Enablers and Inhibitors of Business-IT Alignment," *Communications of the Association for Information Systems,* vol. 1, no. 11, 1999.

[54] F. Coster, "Business-IT Alignment," 2010. [Online]. Available: https://businessitalignment.wordpress.com/about/. [Accessed 10 02 2017].

[55] Gartner Inc., "IT Strategy: A CIO Success Kit - Gartner Executive Program," 03 2009. [Online]. Available: http://www.emacromall.com/techpapers/IT%20Strategy%20A%20CIO%20Success%20Kit.pdf. [Accessed 14 02 2017].

[56] Stanford University, "Stanford University's IT Services Strategic Plan," 2012. [Online]. Available: https://uit.stanford.edu/strategy/strategicplan. [Accessed 13 02 2017].

[57] University of North Carolina, "2010-2015 University of North Carolina at Charlotte Strategic Plan Template for Information Technology Services," 2010. [Online]. Available: http://itservices.uncc.edu/sites/itservices.uncc.edu/files/media/2010-2015%20Strategic%20Plan%20Template%20ITS.pdf. [Accessed 13 02 2017].

[58] Baylor Business, "Nonprofit Technology Collaboration," 13 07 2013. [Online]. Available: http://www.baylor.edu/business/mis/nonprofits/. [Accessed 13 02 2017].

Author Profile

Prof. Richard Boateng is a technology researcher who focuses on developing, promoting and protecting ideas and concepts into sustainable projects of commercial value and development impact. Richard is an Associate Professor in information systems at the University of Ghana Business School. Richard serves as the Head of the Department of Operations and Management Information Systems at the business School.

Richard is also the associate editor of the Information Technologies & International Development Journal and serve on the editorial board of the Information Development Journal. His research experience covers e-learning, information and communication technologies (ICT) for development, electronic governance, social media, electronic business, gender and technology, mobile commerce, and mobile health at the national, industrial, organisational and community levels.

His research work contributes to the over 30 publications he has published on ICT adoption and usage in developing country contexts. He also has expertise in policy development and led a team to develop the University of Ghana guidelines for industry engagement and technology commercialisation. Since joining the University of Ghana in 2010, Richard has collaborated with other faculty to obtain not less than 1.2 million USD in research and project funds. These research and project funds have been obtained from organisations including Vodafone Group (global), Danish International Development Agency (DANIDA), International Development Research Centre (Canada), and the World Bank. Richard has also consulted for the United Nations Development Programme (UNDP), Ghana and United Nations Educational, Scientific and Cultural Organisation (UNESCO) Accra Cluster Office on technology and communication development projects.

Richard has a doctorate degree in Development Informatics and a master's degree in Management and Information Systems from the University of Manchester, UK. He is a British Chevening Award Scholar and a Dorothy Hodgkin Postgraduate Award Scholar. In March 2011, Richard received the Southern University (USA) Research Leadership Award, for contribution to ICT Research in Africa, awarded at the 4th International Conference on ICT for Africa, 26 March, 2011, held at Covenant University, Ota, Nigeria. Richard can be reached by richard@pearlrichards.org. His recent Global Report on Inequalities and Access to Communication can be accessed at http://goo.gl/IgzVB4

Index